FOREVER
IN
Faith

Forever in Faith
Copyright © 2015 by Tfutza Publications
ISBN: 978-1-60091-383-9

Tfutza Publications

P.O.B. 50036
Beitar Illit 90500
Tel: 972-2-650-9400
Tfutza1@gmail.com

First printed in Hebrew as: Ma'alot Mitachat L'efes
Cover Design: Aviad Ben-Simon

Distributed by:
Israel Bookshop Publications
501 Prospect Street
Lakewood, NJ 08701
Tel: (732) 901-3009
Fax: (732) 901-4012
www.israelbookshoppublications.com
info@israelbookshoppublications.com

Printed in Israel

Distributed in Europe by:
Lehmanns
Unit E Viking Industrial Park
Rolling Mill Road,
Jarrow, Tyne & Wear NE32 3DP
44-191-430-0333

Distributed in Australia by:
Gold's Book & Gift Company
3- 13 William Street
Balaclava 3183
613-9527-8775

Distributed in S. Africa by:
Kollel Bookshop
Ivy Common
107 William Rd, Norwood
Johannesburg 2192
27-11-728-1822

Distributed in Israel by:
Shanky's
Petach Tikva 16
Jerusalem
972-2-538-6936

FOREVER IN *Faith*

THE SASSOVER REBBETZIN REFLECTS

BY REBBETZIN BLUMA TEITELBAUM WITH B. COHEN

INTRODUCTION

Both mother and son were listening intently to the recorded voice coming from the tape deck as it described the riveting story of a Holocaust survivor. The mother was Rebbetzin Bluma Teitelbaum of Sassov, *a"h*, and the son *yblct"a*, the Sassov-Monsey Rebbe, *shlita*.

"And what about you?" the Rebbe asked his mother. "You, too, have a story, one that has yet to be told. Maybe you can tape your memories, and they will remain as a testament for future generations."

As he spoke, the Rebbetzin suddenly saw before her an image of her kitchen in Eretz Yisrael, in Kiryas Yismach Moshe. On the counter was a pen and a notebook, but the pages of the notebook were blank.

"Ima, please! Write down at least some of your memories," her children had pleaded on so many occasions. "You went through so much, you had so many close encounters with death, and you survived, *b'chasdei Hashem*, thanks to many miracles. But we don't have any tangible record of those years—surely something should be preserved, to pass on to the next generation? Something that will show them how it is possible to prevail against Amalek and to rebuild a true Jewish life."

Hoping she would take their words to heart, they had placed a notebook and pen on the kitchen counter, in order for her to jot down memories whenever they surfaced.

But the pages had remained blank. How could simple pen and ink express the emotions of those years? How could paper contain them? How, indeed, could words ever come close to capturing what the Holocaust was and what it had done to Hashem's precious Jews?

Time passed and the tales remained untold.

Until 1990.

Following a complicated operation, the Rebbetzin was recuperating in her son's home in America. On Tishah B'Av, the day of the *Churban*, the Rebbetzin started to recount her story. Over the space of a few weeks, the stories were taped; now there would be a lasting memory.

Six years of unimaginable suffering now found expression, through simple words and sentences describing the contrast between darkness and light, between depraved cruelty and extraordinary compassion, between the *Am Segulah* and a nation that sought to eliminate Hashem's Name from the world.

Amid the horror and degradation of daily life under the Nazis, *yimach shemam*, a group of girls bound themselves together in order to preserve their allegiance to the *Ribbono shel Olam*. Their characters were forged in homes of Torah and in the Bais Yaakov schools they attended before the war, and they did not compromise their values even when circumstances demanded of them superhuman strength. Even in the camps, their discussions centered around the *halachos* relevant to the nature of their trials; even on the Death March, their focus was on what the Torah demanded of them at that moment.

The Rebbetzin's words are inspiring, uplifting, truly above this world—and yet, the written words on paper fail to convey the tone of her voice, the utter submission to the Divine Will that was her trademark. Even when her voice became choked with tears, she continued to speak, convinced that her task at that moment was to transmit her experiences to others that they might learn from what she had endured. And even when the emotions were overwhelming, never did she express even the slightest hint of refusal to accept even this as *ratzon Hashem*. *"Gvul samta, bal ya'avorun"*—Hashem set a boundary that they may not cross. To feel pain—yes. To question—never.

This is the spirit in which the Rebbetzin's memoirs were penned, the spirit of the eternal Jew, forever bowing his head in submission to the Divine plan of which he is part. May we merit to find in her words the encouragement we need to persevere in our own lives and struggles and to focus solely on serving Hashem in spite of—and because of—everything.

The righteous Sassover Rebbetzin *a"h* was the daughter of the esteemed *chassid*, HaRav Yosef Strom of Tarnow, *Hy"d*, and the wife of the Sassover Rebbe, *ztvk"l*, founder of Kiryas Yismach Moshe. She was the sole survivor of her illustrious family.

Her righteous sons are: the Sassover Rebbe-Kiryas Yismach Moshe *shlita*; R' Chanoch Henoch Teitelbaum *shlita*, the Sassov-Monsey Rebbe; R' Moshe Teitelbaum *shlita*, Dayan and Moreh Tzedek of Khal Yitav Lev of Satmar-Yerushalayim; HaRav Shlomo Teitelbaum *shlita*, Rebbe of Alesk-Yerushalayim; her daughter, Rebbetzin Esther Rabinowitz *tlita*, and her son-in-law HaRav Dovid Manish Rabinowitz *shlita*, the son of the Biala Rebbe, *shlita*.

May the name of her daughter-in-law, Chana Mindel *bas* HaRav Eliyahu Yehoshua Geldzahler *shlita*, be remembered for a blessing. Chana Mindel *a"h* was the first wife of the Sassov-Monsey Rebbe. She was *niftar* at a young age, after tremendous suffering, on 26 Sivan 5771. During the illness of her mother-in-law, the elder Sassover Rebbetzin, Chana Mindel devoted herself entirely to her care, and her extraordinary devotion will never be forgotten.

This book will surely take its pride of place among the accounts of Jews who rose above the despair and depravity of the Holocaust; Jews who provide us with living, vibrant examples of the nobility of our People and our capacity to serve Hashem with all our hearts, all our souls, and all our might.

1

Against the Tide

T he knocking at the door was loud and staccato. I opened
the door and fell silent.

Who are these people? Shaindy and Mire'le? I wondered
to myself. *What happened to them?* Something in their gaze was
estranged and distant. Their eyes burned with an unfamiliar
flame, and their style of dress—it was so different…

"Call Chaya," Shaindy demanded, drumming her fingers
impatiently.

Chaya came to the door, and the same surprised look crossed
her face. She, too, had a hard time recognizing the girls,
daughters of prominent families in Tarnow whose fathers were
G-d fearing Yidden.

"Come outside for a minute," Mire'le winked at my sister.

Chaya slowly followed the two girls. I stepped onto the
balcony and followed them tensely with my eyes. I saw them
explain something to Chaya with animated hand motions. Chaya

continued to express reserve; I saw that she was not convinced by whatever they were saying. After a few minutes, she came back inside, her eyes full of tears.

"Mama," she said in a choked voice to my mother, who was bent over her sewing machine. "Can I speak to you?"

I had a hard time falling asleep that night. In my young heart I understood that something dangerous was simmering beneath the surface. In my mind's eye I could see the images of good girls who had joined various youth movements that had cropped up in Poland. "Let my dear older sister not get swept up," I *davened* in my heart for Chaya. "I can't think about it, her looking like…like a *shiksah, chas veshalom*."

The next day, I noticed the Friedman girls chatting in the street with Necha. Again, I felt a chill of fear tingle up my spine. All of Tarnow knew that Leika and Malka Mattele Friedman had joined the Socialists. What did they want from Necha, for goodness sake?!

That evening, Mama updated Tatte about the efforts of girls in the city to tempt Chaya and Necha to join those foreign movements. Tatte was horrified, and my brother Mordechai, a *bochur*, was similarly shocked.

"I think," Tatte said in a firm tone, "that we will have to seriously consider the new idea, a vision that is beginning to take hold."

"Tatteh means the idea of Bais Yaakov," Mordechai explained.

I was a little girl, in elementary school, and I went to sleep early at night. But again, I could not fall asleep; I listened to the conversation from my bed.

I knew that some *gedolei Yisrael* objected to the idea of Bais Yaakov. Even great rebbes and *rabbanim* had raised doubts about this new movement and those standing behind the initiative. But Tatteh and Mordechai were right, of course; the fear of being ensnared by the winds that were sweeping through the streets tipped the scales in favor of Bais Yaakov. My parents realized that the answer to the problem was Bais Yaakov, the major breakthrough of that generation.

A few days later, Mama went to the apartment where the Bais Yaakov was housed. She registered her four daughters who were of school age.

And that's how I, Bluma Strom, was privileged to be accepted with great excitement and joy to the first grade, taught by Morah Gittel Laufer. My wonderful teachers taught me Chumash, Yahadus, Neviim, and Kesuvim, and many other lessons that were like music to my ears.

In the mornings I still attended the Polish school, which was mandated by law, but in the afternoons, I would sit and drink in the Jewish studies in Bais Yaakov.

Speeches In Honor of Poland

Little Rivky's cries filled the house. Her face was red, and her hands and legs flailed restlessly. I hurried over to the cradle.

"Blumka, go rock Rivka'le!" my mother asked, as she went out to bring in the dry laundry.

I'll be late, I said to myself, and the image of the Polish teacher rose in my mind. *But the teacher won't be angry. I'll tell her I was putting the baby to sleep. She'll forgive me, like she always does.*

The teacher was a strict non-Jewish woman, and an anti-Semite. I sensed that she was angry at us, the Jewish girls, because we were more capable and talented than the Polish girls in the class. We excelled at recitation by heart and in writing. We even knew the Polish language better than the Polish girls!

Every so often, I was late for school. My parents were extremely busy, my brothers learned Torah in *cheder* and yeshivah, and I helped with the rocking. That is how babies were raised then—they were either picked up or rocked in the cradle.

The door opened and I leaped happily from my place. "Oh, Marisha is here!" I cried.

The elderly non-Jewish woman who worked for us entered, a toothless smile on her face. She automatically walked over to the cradle. Marisha didn't know how to do anything other than rocking the baby's cradle, but it was a huge help!

I arrived late at school. "Why are you late?" the teacher asked me with a piercing stare.

I said the truth: "I was rocking my baby sister's cradle."

Again the teacher forgave me, despite her unconcealed hatred for Jews.

"Where is your sister Chaya?" she asked. "Why didn't she come? Go and call her!"

I happily re-emerged into the pleasant sun and walked home slowly to summon Chaya to school. Without the talented Strom girls, the Polish teachers just didn't manage!

Who, for example, spoke before the class on special national dates in Poland? Me—Bluma Strom. The teacher often gave me the honor of speaking before the girls. On the non-Jewish holidays and patriotic holidays, she would call me out of class and say, "I want you to speak about the importance of the day, in honor of our dear land, Poland!"

I was a good speaker from a very early age, and I always agreed to the teacher's request. Without even preparing, I was able to speak to the class about the "auspiciousness" of the day.

Poland lost its independence in 1795. Three countries took over parts of it: Germany (Prussia at the time) got a small part, and the two other large parts were taken over by Austria and Russia. The western part of the country, controlled by Austria, was called Galicia by the Jews, while the eastern part was called "Congressional Poland." The non-Jews on the Galician side received a more western education, while the Russian side was very primitive.

The city of Tarnow was considered part of Galicia. Until World War I, it belonged to Austria. After the war, it was transferred to Polish control, but the Galician style remained ingrained in the Jews of Tarnow.

Between the two world wars, Tarnow was home to more than twenty thousand Jews who belonged to various communities. The chassidic *presence was very prominent. Many important rebbes and their* chassidim *lived in the city, and on Shabbos, they walked majestically with their* bekeshes *and* shtreimlach.

By contrast, many Jews in Tarnow were affiliated with different movements. There were Communists, Socialists, Yiddishists, Bundists, and of course, Zionists.

Regretfully, masses of the youth became ensnared by these movements. The young Jews of Poland, who were brilliant and talented, wanted to "progress" and to "become educated." They followed the winds of the Socialist Left, and even girls from chassidic *homes began following those errant paths.*

How many tears were spilled, how much heartache there was! Chassidic *bochurim and girls from G-d fearing homes were lost to their parents and cut off all contact with traditional Yiddishkeit.*

"Children, please take out papers! Each child should write down who they think is suitable to be class president!" the teacher called.

Each year, this would repeat itself, and a Jewish president was always chosen, because the Jewish children were the most talented.

My teacher couldn't tolerate Jews, and therefore, she would add, "In our class there will be two presidents—one Jewish and one Polish. I ask each child to write down two names, as per my instructions!"

The same anti-Semitic teacher went even further when I was in seventh grade.

One day, she announced that she was establishing a "ghetto" in the classroom. Of course, she didn't say it clearly as that, and she acted in an ostensibly diplomatic and dignified fashion.

"All the Jewish pupils please move to one row," she instructed, her voice dripping with arrogance.

In response to our questioning looks, she explained: "The Jewish children behave better than the Polish ones and I want the Polish pupils to learn from them. Therefore, the Jews will sit separately from the Poles!"

Perhaps she felt a need to apologize for her anti-Semitic actions, and therefore added an even more detailed explanation: "The Polish pupils talk and disturb, and if I separate the Jewish students, everyone will see where the noise comes from, and this way the Polish children will learn from the Jews how to behave."

It was a lie. She had instituted the "ghetto" out of pure hatred for us!

We Jewish pupils moved together and felt very humiliated. It was clear that she planned to pick on us.

In the afternoon, when we went to Bais Yaakov, we told everyone what had happened.

The response was total shock! The news spread fast; Bais Yaakov was a recognized movement led by the heads of Agudas Yisrael, and when they heard this story, they were furious.

Apparently, pressure was applied from higher up for the teacher to annul this arrangement, because one day she announced, "Children, I see that the Jewish children have no influence on the Poles in any case, and therefore, we are going to move back to the old seats."

My Home in Tarnow

I had a warm, loving home. My dear father was the renowned *chassid* R' Yosef Strom, *Hy"d*, and my beloved mother, Esther, *Hy"d*, was the daughter of a *dayan* and *talmid chacham*.

We were direct descendants of the "Sifsei Chachamim," who also lived in Tarnow, and whose name was Strom. The Strom family was large and respected with a distinguished lineage, and all its descendants are related.

We were nine children:

Raizel Leah, *Hy"d*, my oldest sister, was married to our cousin HaRav Avrume'le Strom, *Hy"d*, a tremendous *talmid chacham* who studied together with the rav of the city. His father was HaRav R' Shmuel Strom, my father's brother. Raizel got married the year before the war began. Hashem took them from us even before they had children.

Necha Breindel, *Hy"d*

Chaya, *Hy"d*

Mordechai, *Hy"d* (about whom I will share a miraculous story)

Sarah Baila, *Hy"d*

Moshe Yehoshua, *Hy"d*

Rivka, *Hy"d*,

and the youngest, **Leibe'le**, *Hy"d*.

I, Bluma, was fifth in the family, born after Mordechai. We all lived in a two room house, one room of which served as a kitchen, and the second, as the dining room and bedroom.

We were a warm, united family, blessed with many talents. I loved my precious family, all of whom perished during the Holocaust, and whenever I speak of them, I am overcome with memories and longing.

Their images accompanied me throughout my eventful life, as I will share with you...

2

THE REBBE'S BRACHOS

O n Shabbos afternoon, my brother Mordechai was playing with a needle. Somehow, he swallowed it, and it began to make its way through his body.

I'll just ignore the needle, my brother, a *bochur*, decided, and went
out like he did every Shabbos to the Belzer *shteibel* in our city.

My parents were ardent Stutchiner *chassidim*. We were extremely
close to the the Rebbe of Stutchin, Rav Yitzchak Horowitz, *zt"l*,
the son of the famed Rav Moshe of Rozvadov, who was a direct
descendant of Rav Naftali of Ropschitz, *zt"l*. The Stutchiner Rebbe
had served as the *sandak* at Mordechai's *bris*.

Mordechai became a Belzer *chassid* as a youth. The Belzer
Chassidus was large and influential in Tarnow; many youngsters
joined, including my brother.

As the hours passed, the needle began to make my brother
very uncomfortable. It poked his internal organs, and he was
doubled over in pain. On Motzaei Shabbos, he could not even

walk home from the *shteibel* and was taken home in a cart.

All the hospitals were closed on Motzaei Shabbos, so we waited for Sunday. All night, Mordechai writhed in pain, and at dawn, my parents took him to the Jewish hospital, where the doctor took an x-ray. They found the needle at a specific point and decided that surgery was called for immediately.

"We will ask the Rebbe!" my parents decided. They didn't dream of signing the consent form for the surgery before asking the Stutchiner Rebbe.

My father went to the Rebbe to mention Mordechai's name for a *brachah* before the surgery. But the Rebbe cried adamantly: "Operate?! *Chalilah!* Travel to Krakow right away!"

My father returned to the hospital with the Rebbe's answer: "We don't want to operate," he said firmly.

The doctor looked at my father like he was mentally unstable. "You have to take him into the operating room this minute! Otherwise, you are playing with your son's life!" he warned.

But my father trusted the Rebbe more than the doctor, and my brother left the hospital and headed for Krakow.

We had an aunt who was a pharmacist who lived in Krakow. She had connections with higher-up places, and any time we needed to exercise *protektsia* with the authorities, she was able to do it for us. Sunday was the official day of rest, but because of our aunt and her connections, Mordechai was accepted for treatment.

The doctor in Krakow was shocked. "Who operates because of a needle?! From the moment the x-ray is taken until the surgery is done, the needle continues to meander through the body, and therefore it is forbidden and superfluous to operate!"

"So what does the doctor suggest we do?" my father asked, looking compassionately at his suffering son.

"Let him stay here in Krakow until things work out," the doctor said.

Mordechai remained at an apartment in the city. Two days

later the needle came out itself, just as the Rebbe had said, with no surgery.

We kept the needle as a symbol of the miracle Mordechai had experienced.

Such miraculous stories, which occurred in the merit of the Rebbe, were abundant in our home, because he was a tremendous tzaddik.

The Rebbe served in the rabbinate in Stutchin from 5644/1884 until World War I. After the war, he settled in our city, Tarnow.

My father and brothers *davened* in his *bais medrash*. Tatte was a leather dealer, and as such, he had a special job: to prepare the Rebbe's chair (the *"shtiel"*), which was made of beautiful leather. My uncle and our *mechutan*, R' Shmuel Strom, *z"l*, of Bochnia, was very close to the Rebbe. He was a renowned *baal tefillah* with a sonorous voice.

On special occasions, when our Uncle Shmuel came to the Stutchiner Rebbe, he was honored with *davening* for the *amud* or singing at *Shalosh Seudos*. His son, my brother-in-law, Reb Avrume'le, an erudite scholar, was also a Stutchiner *chassid*.

At a young age, Mama experienced a great miracle through one of the *tzaddikim* of the generation.

When she was fourteen, she was orphaned of her parents. She moved to the home of her grandfather, a prodigious *talmid chacham*. Good Jews cared for her and sent her to learn a skill, sewing. When she concluded her studies, she began to earn a living as a seamstress.

My mother's tranquil days in her grandfather's house did not last long. He also passed away in the prime of his life and she was left alone. Several residents of the city became my mother's official custodians.

At that time, it was very hard for a girl without a dowry to marry; therefore, Mama made sure to deposit whatever she earned with one of her guardians, so the money that accumulated would be a dowry for her.

One day, a new seamstress moved into the building where Mama worked. The seamstress was located at the outer side of the building, so customers on the way to Mama's store entered her workshop instead. At first they did so out of curiosity, but ultimately they got stuck there and made their orders with the new seamstress.

My mother traveled to one of the Rebbes who lived near Reisha to tell him that her livelihood was in jeopardy. When she wanted to enter, the *gabbai* told her, "The Rebbe has no time to see you now. He is preparing to travel."

Mama did not give up. She pleaded, saying that she was an orphan and, as such, requested to please speak to the Rebbe.

When the tzaddik heard this, he instructed that she be granted entry.

Mama wrote a *kvittel* and entered the Rebbe's chamber. She told him about the good income she had been earning, and that she was saving money for a dowry when the time came, but now a new seamstress had moved into the same building and was robbing her of her livelihood.

"Go home, go home!" the Rebbe replied. "*Vest shoin matzliach in alle ofanim* (you will succeed in all areas). She won't bother you anymore!"

And how did this *brachah* come to fruition?

A cat somehow got into the other seamstress' house and drove her crazy wherever she went. All kinds of tactics and efforts to be rid of it were for naught! When the seamstress realized that she could not get rid of the cat, she had no choice but to move to another apartment. Mama's previous status was restored and she saw much success in her work.

With the Rebbe's Granddaughters

It was early, and I heard Tatte's voice penetrating my dreams.

I jumped up and remembered right away: It was Simchas Torah! We had to hurry to the Rebbe's *bais medrash*, where we would wait until *hakafos*. Tatte would seat us on the window over the Rebbe's private room before *davening* started. We would sit near the Rebbe's granddaughters for the entire *davening*, waiting patiently for our excellent view of the *hakafos*!

I was a young girl when I walked with my sisters and father early in the morning to the *bais medrash*. There were two small barred windows in the ladies' section, and it was very hard to see through them to the men.

I remember the *hakafos* as a lofty, wondrous event. The large *bais medrash*, which was built just a few years earlier, was packed with hundreds of *chassidim*. The Rebbe danced while hugging the *sefer Torah* fervently, and the crowd danced and sang in place, rejoicing with the Torah. *Bochurim* stood on the tables and benches in organized rows, singing and clapping enthusiastically as the rebbe danced round and round with great joy.

The pinnacle of the *hakafos* was when the Rebbe danced to the special *niggun* of the Ropschitz dynasty, *Tzemach Bemalchus*. The *niggun* still echoes in my mind after all these years. I can see the Rebbe dancing and swaying with the *sefer Torah*, enveloped in a holy aura...

The Stutchiner Rebbe passed away in the city of Sanok on 24

Adar while fleeing from Tarnow. He could not withstand the travails of the journey. *Hashem Yikom Damo*.

Mordechai Goes to Belz

It was evening, two nights before Shavuos. There was a knock at the door, and we hurried to ask, "Who is it?"

"We're from the Belzer *shteibel*," was the reply. "Mordechai is about to depart on a train to Belz (at the time, a special train was arranged for all those traveling to Belz). Please take out his Shabbos clothes, some shirts, and cheesecake."

Mama, an ardent follower of the Stutchiner Rebbe, went over to the cupboard, took out several shirts, Mordechai's *bekeshe* and *gartel*, and packed up some cheesecake. As her hands worked, her eyes were bright at the thought that Mordechai had gotten "swept up" into such a wondrous place as the Belzer Chassidus.

3

THE GROUND TREMBLES

"**C**hickens for cheap!"
"Fresh vegetables!"
"Quality fabrics!"
The hawking of the vendors created a babble of noise at the market, with each merchant enthusiastically touting his merchandise.

Thursday and Friday were market day in Tarnow for the locals and for villagers who came from the surrounding areas. After the vendors finished selling, they'd go to buy merchandise in the Jewish-owned stores.

That's the way it was until Hitler, *ym"s*, rose to power in Germany in 5693/1933. After that, even in Poland people began to feel the seething anti-Semitism.

"Long live Poland! We demand economic independence! Don't buy merchandise from the Jews!" the local Poles called to the villagers who wanted to enter the Jewish stores.

The non-Jews had never particularly liked the Jews, but they were at least embarrassed to display their ideologies openly. Hitler, like Amalek in his time, "cooled the tub" and brazenly implemented his ideas publicly. He conducted gatherings in Germany where he disseminated virulent incitement. The surrounding European countries, understanding that there was no longer any reason to fear airing such views, joined the choir of anti-Semites.

Poland also began to persecute its Jews.

The Polish General Pilsudski was a supporter of democracy who was firmly opposed to anti-Semitism and worked for equal rights. At the beginning of World War I, it was he who helped establish an independent Polish country, and formed the Polish Army and the new government. There was real democracy in Poland. Despite the fact that as a general, he did not have the authorities of a head of state— everyone obeyed whatever Pilsudski said. That was all fine and good until Pilsudski died in 1936. His death was a catalyst for anti-Semitism in Poland to explode, and the country joined the choir of the European nations spreading the anti-Semitic spirit.

A Dairy Shabbos

I returned home from school to the aroma of cheese danishes, latkes, and dairy blintzes.

What are all these smells about? I wondered to myself. *Why don't I smell chicken soup and meat for Shabbos?*

All at once, I remembered our conversation with Mama the night before.

"How will we get ready for Shabbos?" my sister had complained. "We're not allowed to eat meat. Are we going to starve all Shabbos?"

I looked at Mama's face. I waited for her soothing explanation that would somehow rationalize the *shechita* decree.

And she explained patiently: "The *gedolei Yisrael* have banned eating meat because of the *shechita* decrees that the authorities want to impose on Poland. The government opposes the Jewish methods of slaughter and they may forbid us to practice them."

Mama dragged the milk barrel into the kitchen. This time, she had bought double the quantity she usually did and we hurried to help her carry the huge, full jug.

"The Jews are the primary consumers of meat in Poland," Mama continued to explain as she spread a dairy tablecloth on the table. "Who needs chickens and geese for Shabbos and Yom Tov if not the Jews?! And who will the poultry sellers lose their money from, if not the Jews?!"

"But don't worry, children," she concluded with a smile. "We will have a *milchig* Shabbos, and it will be delicious and wonderful, you'll see!"

That Shabbos, not a single Jew in Poland ate chicken at their meals. Everyone worked hard as Shabbos approached to prepare dairy delicacies for an elegant menu.

The Polish meat and poultry merchants almost went out of their minds when their coops and barnyards remained full to capacity.

The collective protest against the authorities was partially successful and limited *shechita* was permitted.

In 5698/1938, the authorities in Germany banned shechita. In Poland, too, one of the political parties tried to pass a law that would prohibit Jewish shechita because of "suffering to animals." After some time it emerged that Mrs. Pasterova, a member of the Polish parliament who had proposed the law, was a German spy. In order to deflect attention from herself she had made herself busy with the anti-Shechita law. (When the war broke out, she was discovered and put to death on the first day of the war.)

It was Friday night, 23 Adar 5698/1938 when the Polish Sejm decided to pass the law prohibiting Shechita. *When the news reached the Jewish community, they were shocked. Rav Chaim Ozer Grodzinski of Vilna issued a proclamation, which stated, among other things: "Is it possible that Poland, which has more than three million Jews, will grab the food from their mouths, and tens of thousands of families that were sustained by the meat industry will starve for bread?!"*

In order to enforce the decree, it was necessary for the law to be approved by the Senate. Jews davened *from the bottom of their hearts for the decree to be annulled, as the public would not be able to withstand it. Before Pesach 1939, the members of Agudas Harabbanim of Poland met in Warsaw and decided to launch a meat and poultry strike. Any Jew living in Poland was banned from eating meat products for sixteen days, from 23 Adar until 10 Nissan.*

The Jews obeyed the strike across the board. Even those who were distant from religion didn't consume meat or chicken on those days. Each day, they fasted for half a day and recited Tehillim and Avinu Malkeinu *in all the shuls. The* rabbanim *delivered rousing speeches to reinforce kashrus standards in Jewish homes.*

Jewish shechita *was permitted in a limited fashion, and the absolute ban was supposed to take effect in 1943. Meanwhile, the war broke out in 1939. Until the last minute, the G-d fearing people worked to annul the law and firmly entrench the kashrus standards.*

Not Afraid of the Principal

"Don't dare be absent on the holiday!" the school administration warned us. Pesach was approaching and the Strom girls were being warned and threatened!

The evil winds blowing through Poland did not pass over the school. The Poles danced to the Germans' tune, and happily joined the anti-Semitic fest. But we were good students, and as such, we were spared the wrath of our teachers and classmates.

"I'm not even considering going to school on Pesach!" I declared to my sister. "How can I sit next to the Polish girl Ludmilla while she munches on her roll or snacks on cookies?!"

They shared my sentiments. The threats and warnings the principal had issued did not move us. We stood uncompromising on our principles and did not go to school for the entire week of the holiday.

On Motzaei Yom Tov of Acharon Shel Pesach, each of us hurried to the homes of one of our non-Jewish friends. We asked for their notebooks, filled in the missing material and prepared homework.

"What did we learn when we were absent?" we asked the Polish girls.

"Nothing much…we learned songs and did crafts… We didn't learn a lot and it was wonderful," they replied with a smile.

We knew it! When we were absent from school, the teacher would not teach the important things we had to learn. Without the brilliant Jewish students, she didn't have anyone to talk to!

At the Mercy of the Street

"Can you believe it?" my friend grabbed my hand in horror. "Those Jews were rich as Korach just a few days ago. They lived in Germany in a twelve-room mansion!"

"For goodness sake, what will happen to them here, under the sky?" I shivered for them. "Entire families, fathers and mothers, children big and small, poor things…"

The traumatic incident took place on a Thursday night, October 27, 1938.

During the night, the Gestapo (secret police) officers in Germany raided the homes of Jewish families who were Polish subjects, according to their lists. They threw them out of their homes and transported them by train to within a few kilometers of the border. Here, they ordered them to walk by foot for a few hours in the dark, to the Polish border.

During World War I, Jews fled from Galicia and Poland to Germany. Until the war, part of Poland belonged to Austria, and the other part to Russia. After Poland declared independence and Hitler had come to power, those Jews remaining in Germany found themselves not belonging to any country. The new German government did not want to grant them German citizenship, and the Polish government did not recognize them as citizens of Poland.

Hitler decreed that German residents who had come from Poland had to return to their lands. His impudence and arrogance mounted from day to day, and he was constantly examining the world's reaction to his daring moves. Here and there, some objection was voiced, but nothing more than that.

On that Thursday night, October 27, 1938, the Germans gathered some twenty thousand Jewish men, women, and children, and kept them under heavy guard. On Friday night, they were taken by train towards the Polish border. They were taken off the trains a few kilometers from the border. They had to make the rest of the distance on foot. "You have to accept them," the Germans ordered the Poles.

"We won't take them in," the Poles refused.

For two weeks, the exiles remained homeless. Their terrible situation touched the hearts of the Jewish parties in Poland, namely Agudas Yisrael. Those parties had an influence in the Polish parliament, as they comprised some ten percent of the House. Tremendous pressure was brought to bear on the Polish government to accept the Jews into the country, and the parties promised that the Jewish community would take the exiles under their wing so that they would not become a financial burden on the Polish economy. The pressure worked and the Jews were divided among the different communities, and were the recipients of generous hachnasas orchim.

Some historians and analysts claim that this was another effort by Hitler to gauge the reaction of the world to his cruelty by abandoning tens of thousands of Jews like that. As he had assumed, there were a few very minor objections, but as a whole, the incident passed without any significant response.

The refugees from Germany flooded the streets; they were in a state of fear and terror. We were shocked at the German brutality. We looked compassionately upon the poor Jews who stood homeless in the streets, totally exhausted from their ordeal.

"It's hard to believe that these Jews lived in wealth and comfort until a very short time ago," we said to each other in disbelief. "Just a few weeks ago they lived in huge mansions and now they are at the mercy of other people's kindness!"

The refugees would rattle their many keys in their hands to prove to everyone from what heights the Germans had toppled them, and how much property the evildoers had robbed from them.

The Jewish community welcomed the exiles warmly. Good Jews cooked for them, prepared meals, contributed money, hosted families, and tried to help where they could. Concurrently, we began to "smell" what this Hitler who had risen to power in Germany was all about. A few days before the war, many people received draft notices to the army, and that's when the Poles finally realized the seriousness of the situation.

The girls were enjoying their time in Bnos camp, but the tense parents demanded they be sent home right away, for their own safety.

The counselors cut camp short by a few days and sent us home to our families. We had all begun to sense the fear hovering in the air; it was almost tangible, and boded dangers that at that time, we could not even fathom...

No one could have imagined what was in store for us.

About a year before the war broke out, Hitler captured regions on the Polish and Czechoslovakian border. He was determined to restore to Germany those parts that Poland had "stolen" after World War I (as the result of the "punishment" imposed on Germany at the time).

That was another step Hitler took to test the world's reaction, and to see how ready Poland was for war.

The Polish leaders were narrow-minded and did not realize that Poland was going to get caught up in a horrific war. Instead of planning and arming itself, the government echelons were busy with petty issues and banal laws. In Germany, for several years before the war broke out it was prohibited to throw away even the smallest piece of iron; it all had to be given to recycling centers to build the tremendous war machine. But in Poland, a law was passed just before the war that made it mandatory to paint all the gates of the homes green!

Thus, the Polish authorities preferred to ignore the impending danger, and instead of planning for it, they focused on trivialities.

4

WAR—IS INTERESTING?!

17 Elul 5699/1939

I woke up in the morning to a deafening noise. I washed my hands and hurried to the window to look outside. The skies of the city were black from the countless aircraft.

And suddenly—Boom!!! And another explosion, and another.

I covered my ears with my hands, terrified. I was a seventeen-year-old girl, but I felt so small and lost...

"What is going on?" I ran to my mother tearfully.

Rumors came up from the street. We didn't have a radio at home, but we were well updated, and my mother also was able to tell us, pale-faced, that Poland was in the midst of being invaded by Germany!

The German army came storming into Poland with tremendous force. We lived quite close to the border, and we saw the planes and heard the thunderous explosions and artillery fire.

People ran frantically through the streets, but where were they to run? Where could they go?!

Nothing had been prepared, not bomb shelters, hiding places, or even protective measures. The Polish government had not prepared its citizens for war, and instead had been busy with gates and gardens.

The weak, unprepared Polish army swayed like a drunkard when faced with the powerful German army. The battle for Warsaw, the capital, lasted two weeks, until it fell into German hands. A few days later, we could already see the Polish soldiers, barefoot and with torn clothes, fleeing en masse to—somewhere. We constantly saw them on the run.

About a week before Hitler, ym"s, crossed the border into Poland, the secret conference between the foreign ministers of Germany and Russia was suddenly publicized. At the time, the famed Molotov-Ribbentrop non-aggression pact had been reached. It was signed on 8 Elul 5699, August 23, 1939.

Then Hitler captured Poland until the Russian border, where he suddenly retreated in favor of Russia, which invaded Poland from the east. The agreement lasted two years, and during this time, Russia provided raw materials (grain, metals, coal, fuel, and more) to Germany, and Hitler enriched the German economy while marching toward his goal of conquering the Western world.

On 27 Sivan 5701 (June 22, 1941), the German Army suddenly crossed the border to the east and began to rapidly capture huge swathes of Poland, Ukraine, and Russia.

Stalin, Russia's leader, was in total shock—that very morning, he had dispatched trains loaded with thousands of tons of raw materials from Russia to Germany.

Concurrent to Germany's invasion of Russia, it began annihilating the Jews on a mass scale, beginning in

Eastern Europe. Historians explain that Hitler knew that the local populations in the region were more hostile to the Jews, and this way, he could also test the Western world's reactions to the annihilations. Later, he moved his death machine to the west as well.

One night, we discovered that we had been left with no military guard. The police had dispersed, and all the Polish government officials had fled. The prison was left unguarded and the prisoners walked free.

That night—which I will never forget—we went to sleep trembling in fear and cold. It was a very vulnerable feeling of insecurity, because there was no organized regime to offer us protection. We clearly sensed the words of the *Mishnah* (*Avos* 3, 2): "*Hevei mispallel bishlomah shel malchus,* pray for the welfare of the rulership, for if not for fear of them, people would eat each other alive."

Near our home was a military bakery. People tore the doors down and burst inside, dragging out sacks of flour that they put away for the coming months. We also obtained such a sack.

The next day, the Germans entered Tarnow.

Kol Sasson with the Trumpeting of War

The war landed on us very suddenly. We were unprepared both mentally and technically.

Even on the Friday that the war began, many weddings were held!

In Poland, weddings were customarily held on Friday, except in the city of Krakow. There was a *takanah* in Krakow from the time of the Rema that weddings should not be held on Friday, because of one case where a *chuppah* was held on Erev Shabbos but continued into Shabbos.

Shabbos was conducted normally. The meals were already cooked from Erev Shabbos and everything was ready.

How naïve us girls were. We spoke among ourselves with typical nonchalance: "What's the problem? Finally, we'll experience something unusual and interesting—war!"

None of us dreamed of the tragic future…

We didn't fathom the ramifications of this war, which would exact six million sacrifices that would ascend on High in total purity.

In my blackest dreams I couldn't have pictured my dear family, the illustrious Strom family, eradicated from the face of the earth.

The elders of Tarnow who remembered World War I wept with worry and sorrow, but they, too, had no idea that this time, it would be the absolute decimation of the Jewish community in Europe; that something heinous the likes of which had never been since Creation, was about to occur.

Right from their arrival in Poland, the Germans created terrible trouble. They burst into our home two days after the invasion, and raided many other homes as well. They would shoot indiscriminately. They abducted Jews from the street at random, and particularly sought *rabbanim,* who they arrested. Once in prison, they tortured them brutally, beat them with the butts of their guns and burned their *peyos* and beards with cigarettes.

We received frequent bursts of chilling news: "Fifty Jews were murdered!" "Two hundred Jews were shot!" What for? Nothing. Jewish blood was spilled like water.

War was declared on any Jewish symbol. All the shuls were locked and prayer there was prohibited. The *chadarim* and schools were barred and all regular Jewish activity was suspended.

Jews continued to gather in private homes, and with tremendous risk to their lives, *davened* in small *minyanim.*

We continued to be naïve, not imagining and not wanting to imagine what was in store for us, because we wanted to live.

A few days later we began to realize what was happening. The decrees became more frequent, and the Germans hung huge placards in the streets proclaiming their rules.

From 6 Teves 5700 (December 18, 1939), all the Jews of Tarnow were forced to wear a blue Star of David printed on a piece of white fabric on their sleeve. The Germans would stand in the street, lying in wait for their prey, and if they even suspected that the strip was sewn slightly crooked on the sleeve, or that it was dirty—they would brutally beat the person with rubber truncheons on the head, face, and eyes. Much Jewish blood was spilled this way, and many lost their vision from these beatings. The fiends were also liable to kill someone for this "sin."

Jewish factories and shops were confiscated, merchandise was looted and the situation grew worse from day to day. One of the things we were not allowed to do was wear fur on our clothes or in our coats. We had to remove all the fur from our clothes and submit it to a central collection point. I removed the warm fur lining from my expensive coat, and handed it over with an aching heart.

They also demanded that we give them all our silver and gold. The Jews who thought they would subsist on the possessions they had kept for themselves had to give everything over.

That sad autumn of 1939, while cottony clouds floated over the skies of Tarnow, and the fallen leaves danced in a macabre fashion, all Jewish public activity stopped. Concurrently, the Germans demanded that Jewish committees be formed to run the community; this committee was called the Judenrat. They also demanded that a Jewish police force be established, and the Germans forced the Jews to become police officers.

After a short time, their true intentions became clear—the organization was only meant to enforce the German demands via Jewish emissaries, just like the oppressors in Egypt who appointed Jews and forced them to carry out the satanic orders of the gentiles.

On 27 Cheshvan 5700, the Germans brutally and bloodthirstily burned down the shuls of the city. The city burned, the sky was colored a garish orange, and the Germans kept pouring flammable materials on the flames so that not a trace would remain of the shuls.

There was a *beis medrash* in Tarnow that had been standing for four hundred years, and that, too, went up in flames.

Mama Promises Basya

One day I wasn't feeling well and Basya came to visit me. As soon as she came in, she burst out crying and told me what was bothering her: "It's been so long since we received a single letter from my father and my brother!"

When Poland was invaded, the Germans split the loot with the Russians. Half of the country was taken over by the Germans and Russia took over the other half. The border between the two countries was the San River, which ran through the city of Sanok.

A few months after the war broke out, before the border was hermetically sealed, many Jews fled to the Russian side. A lot of them failed to reach their destinations and were handed over to the Germans. Some of the gentile smugglers tricked the Jews, taking large sums of money to smuggle them to the Russian side—but in the end, turning them in.

Basya's father and brother had tried to flee to the Russian side but had been caught and taken deep into Germany. The family waited for a long time for a sign of life. It was a nerve-wracking wait. In the end they received a letter from the two that said: "We are in a camp in the city of… If you could send us a kilo, or at least half a kilo of bread, or other food…"

Such heartrending letters reached Basya's home every so often.

The day that Basya visited me she cried to me: "We are constantly worrying! Why haven't we received any letters from them?"

Mama listened to Basya's sobs sympathetically, and then held her hand warmly and said, "I promise you, you will soon hear good news!"

My pious mother's promise was fulfilled that very night.

It was very late when Basya's family heard a knock at the gate. The family began to tremble. Who could it be?! No one was allowed to leave their homes after eight o'clock, so there were no Jews outside at all. Who could be at the gate?!

Suddenly they heard pleading voices. "Open, please open! Please!"

The pleas grew louder until the family went to the window and caught their breaths in shock: their father and brother were standing in the courtyard, safe and sound!

It is hard to describe the magnitude of the miracle and the emotional reunion. The two had wondrously managed to secure their release from the camp using a gold pen, which they had "stuck" in the right places. The bribe made it possible for them to be released and return home.

Two years later, the entire family were led to their deaths with the rest of our brethren. Hashem should avenge their blood.

At one point, my father and Mordechai also set out to

smuggle themselves into Russia. Mama accompanied them while we remained at home, waiting apprehensively for her to return. The Stutchiner Rebbe was also part of the group, but his strength gave out in Sanok. There he collapsed and his soul returned to its Maker. It was 24 Adar 5700/1940.

When my parents and Mordechai reached the San River, they could not decide if they would be better off crossing the river or staying. Ultimately they decided to all turn back and return home.

5

As Long As the Pistol is Polished

"**D**o you have a good book?" I asked my friend Mirel. "Yes, I got a great one!" she replied excitedly, and gave me a big fat book with a cover written in Russian. I was happy. I would have what to read to help me forget what was happening all around us.

The already strong bond between my friends and I grew only stronger in those days. Together, we tried to overcome the various difficulties that cropped up because of the new reality. Bais Yaakov was no longer active, nor was Bnos; there was no shul or *bais medrash*. We began to study English and a bit of German on our own, sort of like "getting to know your enemy." We also lent each other riveting books.

It was a Sunday. I was out with my friends, holding the book that Mirel had lent me. We were walking on one specific side of the street because we were not allowed to walk on the other side. We were limited as to where we could live as well; we could only reside on specific streets, which formed sort of an open ghetto.

As we walked, we suddenly heard a bloodcurdling shout: "Stand where you are! Stand where you are!"

Frightened, we turned around and looked.

"*Oy, gevald!*" my friends moaned. "It's the German commander and he's pointing at you!"

I was stunned! Why me? What had I done?! What crime had I committed?! I couldn't think of a single incriminating act...

But the people around me were all pointing at me, and the beast was walking towards me.

I was familiar with every nook and cranny in Tarnow. A few meters away was a coal store. It was gated in, and there was a way to slip out into the yard. *I'll slip in there,* I thought to myself, *and I'll toss the book over the fence. That man must not catch me with the book!* At the time, Germany was at odds with Russia, and woe unto me if he caught me with a Russian language book.

I ran for my life. I tried to sneak into the courtyard, but he caught up to me. The "incriminating" book was still in my hand. I hadn't yet been able to toss it away...

I stood up, both hands behind my back clutching the book.

The evil man looked at me, his face contorted with hatred and cruelty. "Do you know who you have the honor of speaking to?" he growled, showing me the horrible Gestapo insignia—a skull—that adorned his lapels.

"I don't know..." I stammered, going pale.

"You kicked me!" he cried.

"I didn't kick, I didn't do anything..." I gasped. "And if so, please forgive me..."

"I should forgive you?" he screamed, and put his hand in his pocket. He pulled out a pistol and from the other pocket he took out a tissue… At the time, before we knew what a tissue was, the "cultural" Germans already knew. He cleaned his pistol from the dust—another manifestation of the Nazis' pedantic habits. They couldn't kill with a dusty revolver!

People gathered round and I heard them speaking with pity and distress. "*Nebach*, what a young victim, so, so young!"

It was clear that the evil man wanted blood to be spilled there and then. He found reasons to kill innocent people every day. Once he killed a woman who was found with a kilogram of white flour. Another day, a poor woman was caught with a chicken. When he picked on someone, you could be sure the incident would finish with the death of his victim.

The man saw the crowd observing what was unfolding, turned around and called: "Everyone please leave!" In other words, this show is not meant for you!

He took his now cleaned gun, pressed it to my head and asked, "Where should I do it from, here? Where should I shoot, into your head or into your heart?" And he moved the gun down to my heart.

During those heart-stopping seconds, I thought of my Father in Heaven, the *Ribbono Shel Olam*, Master of all souls, in whose Hands lies the soul of every living being!

I was suddenly infused with daring and strength. Thoughts of *emunah* coursed through me powerfully. "If You want to give me more life, dear Father, Tatte *zisser*…" I prayed silently with complete *emunah* and clarity, "then he can't do anything to me, even though the gun is already resting on my heart!"

Amidst my thoughts and my sense of closeness to my Creator, I heard his voice: "Go stand near the wall there with your hands up."

That's how the Germans used to shoot, and he wanted to do the same to me. But *HaKadosh Baruch Hu* put a surprising thought in my mind. Instead of walking over to the wall and raising my hands—I should begin to run!

I burst into a frantic dash. Angels seemed to carry me. I disappeared into the crowd and blended among the people. Furious, he fired into the air, again and again, but my life had been spared.

I fled into a nearby house, where I waited for a long time, until I peeked outside and saw that he was gone.

That entire time, my friends stood at a distance and observed the scene with pounding hearts and mounting dread. They were sure that I had been killed…

Poor girls! They stood there, petrified, and suddenly I walked over to them, safe and sound. I cannot describe the joy with which they fell on me! They hugged and kissed me emotionally. "You have no idea what kind of miracle you just had!" they cried.

After we all recovered a bit, someone glanced at her watch and exclaimed, "It's almost eight o'clock!"

After eight, no Jews were allowed to walk in the streets. Anyone who transgressed this decree was shot to death on the spot.

I ran quickly and arrived home at the last minute. Mama was already pacing worriedly at home murmuring, "Where is my Bluma'le? Where is Bluma? It's almost eight o'clock…"

I didn't tell anyone what had happened. I was terrified that if I would, panic would descend on the house and any time someone would be late again, Mama would fret terribly because who knew what had happened.

What will happen if the fiend meets me again? I worried. *He will want to take revenge!*

I found a solution: I changed my hairstyle a bit, hoping that if he would see me in the street he would not recognize me.

Somewhere in the Forest

We felt the noose tightening around our necks from day to day. Until now, Jews were only allowed to live on one side of the city and weren't allowed to leave their homes at night. On 17 Teves 5701, the beard and *peyos* decree was issued.

During Adar I 5701, the ghetto was formed. In Sivan, Jews from the entire region were moved to Tarnow and the number of Jews in the ghetto reached 40,000. The gate of the ghetto was closed and locked and we were caged into prison. No one went in or out.

The Germans established a headquarters with Jewish police officers to help them. One of them, Horowitz, was reputed to be making an effort to save as many Jews as he could, and he saved us once also with his wisdom.

Later, when *aktions* began and the sadists ran wildly from house to house to flush out those who were hiding, Horowitz would run with them. If he saw a pair of legs peeking out from beneath a cupboard, from inside it, or from the crawlspace, because the poor person could not hide himself properly, he would scream, "Oberstfuhrer, I think I saw a pair of legs peeking out in the other room!"

By doing this, he first distracted the Nazi's attention to another room so he wouldn't notice the legs in the room being searched. In addition, saying this would spur the people to hide themselves better.

Other police officers would warn the Jews about upcoming raids so that they wouldn't walk around in the streets with valuables on their person. If a Jew was found with money in his hand, or food, he was usually shot on the spot.

The Germans weren't familiar with Tarnow and its many streets and paths. Initially, after the ghetto gates were locked, the Jews succeeded in finding breaches and they would either slip through them, or leave through windows or cellars. Our building also had such a breach where we could slip in and out. There was also a pharmacy with two entrances: you went through one door inside the ghetto, and through the second you emerged on the Aryan side. Likewise, you could sneak into the ghetto that way.

Jews who were able to stay out of the ghetto hid under assumed identities with Aryan papers. Every so often, they slipped into the ghetto to obtain money or meet family members. They would come through our building and blend in with us.

One day, a woman came from outside the ghetto and told us sadly, "Don't think, children, that what is happening here is the worst. There is worse going on! Somewhere in the forest, there is a complex surrounded by soldiers and electric barbed wire fences, and anyone who touches the wire, dies on the spot. There's a big sign with the word 'Crematorium' on one of the buildings and no one comes out of there alive…"

We didn't believe her stories. We refused to recognize the horrific reality. But she repeatedly claimed, "This is what they say. They say it's true and it's the fate that awaits us all."

Until that fate arrived we suffered many other travails. People being abducted in the street became a matter of course. We knew that in the town near Tarnow there was a big work camp for men. The Nazis would abduct Jews from the street and send them to the camp.

At first, the Germans let the inmates send letters home, so we knew that the conditions there were very difficult, unbearable. That's not to mention the issues regarding kashrus, Shabbos, and *Yamim Tovim*.

Mesirus Nefesh in the Ghetto

Rosh Hashanah 5702/1941.

Three books were opened, and the words, "Who will live and who will die" were cried from the *machzorim* with great anguish.

More than ever, the Jews in the ghetto felt the need to *daven* together, to plead before the Creator to abolish the decrees.

A *minyan* convened in the building where we lived. The landlord had a *sefer Torah*.

"You will take shifts standing guard at the entrance to the building," we Strom girls were told. We stood watch, our eyes shifting left and right constantly to see if the Germans were approaching. They did not rest on that day, knowing that it was a holiday and a time of prayer for us. They went from house to house, hunting for Jews who were *davening*.

When the Germans approached our building, we quickly warned the worshippers: "They're coming!"

Everyone scattered in fear, dashing into hiding places—one in a cupboard, another in an attic, a third in the bomb shelter. When the Germans burst into our house, they didn't find a single man.

Mama recoiled at the sight of the soldiers. Their faces burned with their lust for murder when they saw that there were no men at home. One of them stamped his boot in anger, and Mama took the beautiful challah off the table and gave it to him. He grabbed it and stomped out of the house.

One day, a friend of mine told me, "My father and brother-in-law are *shechting* for the ghetto's Jews."

"How are they doing that?" I asked in a frantic whisper. It was so dangerous!

She described the risky process: "My sister and I disguise ourselves as gentile girls. We walk to the prearranged meeting place and carry the *chalefs* under our coats.

"We meet with the gentile lady and purchase a lamb from her. Then my father comes, also disguised, wearing a scarf so no one should recognize him, and slaughters the lamb secretly—risking his life so the Jews should have a bit of meat to eat."

The parents in the ghetto were afraid of their children. What were they hearing? If the Germans would catch them and torture them, what would they reveal?

At the time, the black-market trade was thriving. The objective of the Germans was for the residents of the ghetto to die of hunger; only those who worked in factories managed to survive. Because of the terrible hunger, anyone who was able to hide something of value tried to sell it in exchange for food. Others tried their hand at dealing in items such as chairs, books, a watch, and the like. Jews walked in the streets hiding various items beneath their coats, which they intended to sell to non-Jews.

The adults feared that the children might break under pressure and talk about the black-market trade. "They might say things to ears that shouldn't hear them and endanger the entire family!" parents sighed.

Beyond the fear, *chinuch* was the parents' primary concern. Despite the difficulty and dangers, they did not take their eyes off the focus—*chinuch*—for a minute. Time passed and the children were not learning—what would be with them? "We have to establish a study framework for them!"

Out of a desperate need, private *chadarim* began to crop up. One *melamed* learned with the little children while another taught the older children. Thus, the light of Torah shone through the darkness of the Tarnow ghetto.

A Secret Kindergarten in the Ghetto

My sister was a preschool teacher in Bais Yaakov until the war broke out. Now that everything had stopped, the girls were idling the days away, and several mothers asked her to operate a secret kindergarten, free of charge.

And so the class opened in the ghetto, under the direction

of the Strom girls. We had several small tables at home that we had been able to take at the last minute from the Bais Yaakov before the Germans impounded it. Now we used them for our "kindergarten." We sat with the girls and told them about the *parashah*, we taught them Yiddish, math, reading, writing, and more.

With time, more and more children joined the class. When summer came, the gentile Polish children frolicked in the playgrounds while the children of the ghetto could not even walk outside freely. We pitied the poor children and decided to take them out to the park adjacent to the German soldiers' bakery, which bordered on our house.

I don't know how we weren't afraid to do it! It was a tremendous risk. We smuggled small groups of children into the locked garden, relying on miracles as we slipped inside. Our lips murmured *tefillos* the entire time, hoping that the soldiers would not notice us. Indeed, Hashem watched over us; neither us nor the children were caught.

Many sad stories remain etched in my mind from the days of the kindergarten. I remember two sisters and a brother who attended. The older girl, who was eight, brought a veritable treasure for breakfast one day: white (not black!) coffee. For some reason, it suddenly spilled and she began to cry heartrendingly.

"Why are you crying?" I asked her.

She replied tearfully: "I am not so upset about the bit of coffee that spilled and that I didn't get to drink...but if Morah would know how much my mother ran around until she got a bit of milk...then she came home and called to us happily: 'Children, today you'll have white coffee, with milk! We took the coffee to kindergarten, and now that little bit spilled...I can't stop crying when I think of my mother's efforts...'"

Such was the life of the children in the ghetto.

One day, around the time of the first *selektion*, we decided to photograph the children. I took the photos with me when we were deported and hid them in my socks and they came with me throughout the Gehinnom I experienced, until they were stolen from me, as I will share later on.

The kindergarten lasted quite a long time, and eventually grew to eighty children. None of them survived. May Hashem avenge the blood of the pure children who had never sinned, who were sacrificed like a *korban olah* and rose straight to the Heavens.

6

MIRACLE AT THE SEWING WORKSHOP

A mild odor emerged from the kitchen, but it quickly dissipated in the wind.

I sat with my sisters in the room as we sadly analyzed the situation. Each one tried to guess what was in store for us, and what the Germans were planning. Suddenly, we made an emotional pledge: "We'll never let them separate us! We'll tie ourselves to each other with rope, and they won't be able to disconnect us!"

It was a moment of sweet dreaming that had no chance of becoming reality... They were the words of naive girls who had no concept of the depths of the barbarism and evil that those seemingly human beings possessed.

Had we known...had the Jews of the ghetto dreamed of their bitter end, perhaps they would have made every effort to flee from the valley of death, to escape to Hungary, which was still free, or to hide under an Aryan alias.

But we didn't know. We sat and talked, not imagining that what was waiting for us was much worse than we could possibly fathom.

Some time later, the men were forced to enlist for work camp; then the women had to do the same. Our family name, Strom, began with an S, and being at the end of the alphabet, I waited a long time for my turn.

Chaim Weissman Helps Out

Sivan 5702/1942.

The ghetto was crammed with 40,000 Jews, many of whom had come in transports from nearby towns.

A few days before the first *aktion*, it seemed the air was aflame. The smell of explosives hung in the air. SS and Gestapo forces suddenly flooded the streets, and we trembled in fear for our lives.

Friends that I knew from Bais Yaakov arrived in Tarnow on transports from places such as Krakow, Katowitz, Bilitz, and others. They had organized work and I wanted to be in their company.

On one of those "burning" days I entered the house with a request. "Mama, I would like to register for work, in the place where my friends are working. They joined the workers in a sewing workshop, where they sew uniforms for German soldiers."

My mother heard me, grasped my hand and cried emotionally, "In days like these, we have to listen to what the children want, and to immediately try to put those wants into action! Come, let's go to our neighbor, Chaim Weissman, to register."

Chaim's mother, Leicha (Leah) Weissman, had lived in the

apartment near ours for twenty-five years, until the establishment of the ghetto. We were very close to the Weissmans, and in normal times, we lived almost as one family.

Chaim Weissman was a good person. He worked for the authorities, and was one of the people in charge of the German uniform sewing workshop. In his capacity, he could use *protektsia*, and my mother wanted to take advantage of that fact. She grasped my hand and we went to the Weissman home.

My mother spoke to Chaim. "Listen, Chaim! My Bluma'le came home with a decision. She said she wants to register to work at the uniform workshop. I am asking you, take the girl, take her to the workshop, and don't send her home! Please take care of this matter for us."

Chaim did not forget the longstanding friendship between the families, and he also greatly admired my mother. He took me right away to the workshop, which was located in the building that had formerly housed Tarnow's *cheder*. When the ghetto was formed, the building was expropriated by the Germans and turned into a uniform factory for the Nazis.

The administrative offices were on the top floor of the building, and the tailors worked one floor beneath that. We went up and that was when we discovered that the workers of the shop were being sent to Krakow.

Chaim stood rooted to his place in shock. How would he return to my mother without having fulfilled her request?!

Chaos reigned as the workers got ready for the transport. People were dashing back and forth, their faces panicked. One ran into a room while a second one ran out. Everyone was waving their hands and talking in confusion. Only Chaim stood stonily in place.

"Why are you standing here?!" someone asked him. "Are you late for the transport of sewing workshop workers? Go downstairs. The Tarnow tailors are there. The factory is going to continue working on a smaller scale."

In peacetime, there were ready-made clothing factories in Tarnow, staffed by socialist tailors. When the war broke out, many of them began to work for the Germans. The day I came with Chaim, a transport of workers departed for Krakow, and the factory that remained in Tarnow now needed additional workers to complete the quota.

Now Chaim understood what we had to do and he went down to the lower floor with me; we entered the tailors' workshop.

"I brought you an expert seamstress!" Chaim Weissman said in Yiddish to one of the people in charge there.

I flushed bright red. I didn't know the first thing about sewing!

I wasn't the only one who had come to the workshop without even the most basic skills. The gentile managers of the veteran workshops in Tarnow had become the managers of the uniform factories, and in this capacity, they put their sons to work, even if they had no sewing skills. They learned on the job and were able to be integrated into the factory's work.

But I was just a "lousy Jew," not the daughter of a gentile manager. I stood, fearful for my fate, and was unable to deny and speak up to say that Chaim was lying.

I was accepted right away. They registered me and then a person told me to follow him. He led me to a huge hall which thundered with the noise of sewing machines. The machines were lined up on the two parallel walls of the hall. Beside each machine sat one tailor with five assistants, girls or boys, who were supposed to help him.

"I brought you an expert seamstress!" the supervisor called out as he approached one of the tailors with me in tow.

The tailor looked me up and down suspiciously. Apparently, I did not match my description.

"Do you know how to sew well?" he asked, his eyebrows knitted together.

"Yes, yes!" I replied with a pounding heart.

"So sit!" he invited me and handed me a military jacket and a needle and showed me what I had to do.

I had never even been able to thread a needle efficiently, something that is a trademark of any expert seamstress or tailor.

As I feared, my threading did not go particularly well. The tailor looked at me and hissed cynically, "Oh, ho, girl, you can't even thread a needle? Some 'expert' you are!"

"I have sewn in the past, but since then, I forgot how to do it!" I replied, my heart fluttering in fright.

He fixed me with that suspicious look again and then jeered, "Really?! When did you have time to learn to sew, then sew and finally, to forget?!"

These confounding questions placed me at great risk. I felt the ground burning beneath me and that I was living on borrowed time.

And then the miracle happened. A dignified looking person suddenly entered the hall and announced to all the tailors: "Put everything down! Senior German army officials are about to arrive and we all have to gather in the auditorium!"

What a miracle! I breathed a sigh of relief, sensing that my life had been handed to me as a gift.

No one spoke anymore of my skills and how much I was (not) able to sew, and the main thing was: I was accepted for work.

I went with everyone to listen to the Germans speak. One of them said that "being that here, uniforms for the Wehrmacht— the wonderful German army—are being sewn (truthfully, the sewing workshop repaired old uniforms), then none of you will be taken for the upcoming *selektion*."

"You Are Also a *Bas Yisrael!*"

The thick, coarse fabric moved slowly beneath the dancing needle.

Needles, needles! That's what I felt in my new workplace. The atmosphere poked my heart until it bled.

The workers, mostly secular and socialist, were very far from a life of Torah, and their outlook was very different than mine. There were a few religious women and men, but the atmosphere was ugly. The tailors spoke of unsavory subjects and in a coarse, base fashion that made me chafe.

I tried to strengthen myself and cleave to Hashem as best I could. Sometimes I was able to *daven* a bit of Shacharis with one friend or another. These *tefillos* gave me the strength to endure the spiritual suffering I experienced; after all, I was just a young girl.

Each day, we were given a bit of food. I tried to leave some for my starving family in the ghetto, and at the end of the day to smuggle them out my portion of food that was left after the distribution.

One day, we were instructed to begin working on Shabbos, but I evaded doing so.

Next to me worked Ziska, a Jewish girl who came from a home where Shabbos was observed, but who was not strong enough to withstand the test. Ziska saw me refusing to work on Shabbos and suggested, "Sit here near me and don't do anything and I will do your work."

"Ziska," I pleaded with her, "Don't speak that way. You are also a *bas Yisrael* and you are not allowed to work for me! You can do as you please, but don't desecrate Shabbos for me…"

But Ziska insisted on "doing me a favor" and didn't let me argue with her…

When Yom Kippur came, I sat in the sewing workshop, very upset at my situation and in the way I was passing the holy day. My yearning for the good days, the days of holiness and purity in the Presence of the Creator, were overwhelming. How had we fallen to such depths?! My heart cried bitterly.

I did not want to desecrate the holy day with work, but the supervisors warned the workers not to dare suspend the work. "The Germans will come specifically today to do an inspection!" they declared. The fiends knew the Jewish calendar very well and were aware that it was Yom Kippur. They made sure to carry out inspections on such days to increase our anguish. Therefore, when the inspection was held, the *frum* ones among us pretended to be working, but we didn't desecrate the holy day.

Hashem had mercy on me and at the end of each day that I spent in the difficult, negative atmosphere, I returned home to my family and friends, where I reinforced my defenses and my strengths. This way, I was able to stick to my principles, without stumbling.

"Oh, Bluma'le, the poor girl of the family," my family bemoaned each time I returned at six in the evening. "Only she has to go out to work…"

At night I would spend time with my beloved friends, and there were also two girls who came to the ghetto from Krakow I became very friendly with. One of them was already taken from me during the first *aktion*.

In the morning, I would return to the workshop, having no other choice. I took a deep breath to gird myself for the day ahead in the company of socialists and secular Jews. The work itself wasn't particularly difficult. The overseer of the workshop was a gentile named Madritch. He treated the workers humanely, and under his watch, we got a better portion of food than the others. I think that he got an award of excellence after the war.

Regretfully, I didn't work under him for long and soon another supervisor arrived.

7

THE HORROR, THE ILLNESS, THE MEDICATION

U ntil the first deportation, we lived in fear and in the shadow of the decrees and harassment. In Sivan 5702/1942, new and chilling horrors began with the dreadful transports and the mass killing.

On 25 Sivan, placards were posted about the "transfer" of some of the Jews to a different place. The Poles were warned not to be in the streets at that time (so that they should not witness the atrocities), and that anyone who was hiding a Jew would be punished by death.

We tried to do everything possible to spare ourselves from the transport. I equipped myself with a stamp from the Gestapo as a worker of the sewing workshop and thus I was able to remain in the ghetto. My father wanted to obtain a similar stamp; he would go from one workplace to another, raise his hands and cry: "I'm a young man, I have two good hands with which to work; I can work well." *B'chasdei Hashem*, he returned home with the coveted stamp.

Jews were allowed to take luggage weighing up to 25 kilograms. Meanwhile we learned that those who had been drafted for the Polish work service had been ordered to dig a long, deep pit in the Jewish cemetery. It is easy to imagine what a horrific feeling spread among the Jews. Their graves were already being dug…

In the afternoon, the streets emptied of people. It was silent as death. Families communed with each other; people wanted to spend their last few hours together. In many homes, there were piles of bundles stacked near the door.

Wrapped in Tallis and Tefillin

26 Sivan 5702, (June 11, 1942)

That morning, I went to work, but my heart pounded in my chest at what was coming. Meanwhile, our ghetto was surrounded by Germans and Ukrainian mercenaries. The Ukrainians wore black; in Polish we dubbed them "*di karaknes*," meaning black worms that evoked revulsion. The Germans burst into homes and issued orders, holding lists in their hands. The Ukrainians executed the shots and the beatings with "exemplary" obedience. Some of the Jews were told where to go while others were shot on the spot. "You are too pretty to remain alive," they declared, and shot. To others, they said, "You're too ugly to live," and then shot.

The city shook from the shooting. Homes filled with dead bodies. The Germans even burst into the work hall where I was and shot at someone who they perceived to have a grey hair on his head. It was atrocity in the fullest sense of the word.

I returned home that evening, trembling and petrified. I told my father what had happened at the workshop.

"If so, it's too dangerous for you to go to work. Tomorrow, you won't go," he said.

All of us remained at home, listening to the shooting. The walls trembled and we heard bloodcurdling shouts of *"Shema Yisrael!"*

It was a dreadful feeling. With the presence of mind of an *oved Hashem*, my father turned to us. "Children, we do not know what the next minute will bring. Let us each say *Viduy*."

They were moments of *teshuvah* and preparation for what was coming. We tearfully recited *Viduy*, and then ran to hide in the cupboard, next to it or under it.

A terrible day of paralyzing fear passed with the shooting and shouting the constant background noise. Finally, the death choir stilled and for now, we remained alive. The next day, my father spoke to us again. "I prefer we don't all stay together in such a small building with just one floor. We have to scatter in several hiding places."

I was sent with two of my sisters to a tiny attic in our building. Through a small window, we were able to look out at what was happening in the ghetto. The entire building shuddered from the gunfire. We gazed fearfully as the stories of *Chazal* about the *churban Bais HaMikdash* came to life before our eyes.

Many Jews who saw what was transpiring wrapped themselves in their tallis and tefillin, preparing to go to the slaughter *al kiddush Hashem*. Cleaving to Hashem and glorifying His Name, the Jews were killed, and then the Nazis dragged them from their homes. Tears streaming down our faces, and chills traveling up and down our spines, we saw how the holy bodies, covered with talleisim, and tefillin wrapped around their arms, were loaded onto carts. Ribbono shel Olam, *look down from the Heavens and see, as we have become a mockery by the gentiles!* The *tefillah* murmured in our trembling hearts.

After a three day reprieve, the *aktion* started up again. The

Nazis demanded that the social department of the Judenrat give them lists of people to send east. Paul Reiss, from the Judenrat, refused and was shot to death, with several of his friends.

More than 20,000 Jews were killed during that *aktion*. Three thousand were shot and killed in cold blood in the city's streets or near the Jewish cemetery; 7,000 were killed in the surrounding forests; 11,500 Jews who did not have working permits were sent to the Belzec concentration camp. The *aktion* began on 26 Sivan 5702 (June 11, 1942), and lasted for nine days, with a three day hiatus in the middle.

The brutal *aktion* left behind empty homes. Entire families had disappeared, and some remained only one third or one quarter intact. Although we all survived, *baruch Hashem*, we were hardly rejoicing. We sat and cried inconsolably, fearing for the worst and knowing that it was only a matter of time until our turn would come.

The ghetto wasn't empty for long, because in the meantime, the Germans were liquidating other ghettos, and right after the deportations, they sent the remaining Jews to the Tarnow ghetto, which once again grew overcrowded. The Tarnow ghetto was among the last ones in Poland to be liquidated.

Hitler refused to recognize Warsaw as Poland's capital, and declared that Krakow, the capital of Galicia, would be the capital. "It is not fitting that Jews should live in Krakow," the district government announced.

"Tarnow, located near Krakow, will absorb all the exiles from Krakow and the entire region!" Once again the ghetto filled with masses of Jews who were refugees from other cities in Poland, until the next deportation.

After the *aktion*, on 14 Tammuz (June 29 1942), we were ordered to move to another ghetto, where we would be hermetically closed in.

We took whatever we could with us. People packed up their entire past in small bundles, dragging sacks, and heading into the dismal future with despondency written all over their faces.

The new ghetto was set within a few streets and it was surrounded by a tall, two-meter wooden fence. The Jewish heads of the ghetto stood at the gates; they had been forced into this guarding task. There were refined people among them who did not want to serve as heads of the ghetto and cause pain to their Jewish brethren, but they could not evade the job. One of them was the officer Horowitz who I mentioned earlier.

Those who went out to work were not allowed to take anything with them. Sometimes the inspections at the gate were only perfunctory and the Jews took the risk of smuggling out items to trade on the black market. They hoped to exchange the items for a bit of food, which they could bring to their starving families.

If the inspection was more thorough, the ghetto heads would come and warn their brethren of what was expected. "Don't take anything; there's heavy guard at the gate and they're looking for people smuggling things!"

But there were other heads who, unfortunately, behaved in a very painful fashion, and we won't speak more about them…

We took up residence in the new ghetto in a house right next to where my sister Raizel lived. A large outdoor balcony connected the two houses. We crowded into the house with the family who had lived there earlier.

The windows of the house looked out onto the plaza where all the *aktions* took place. In the past, it had served as the main bus stop for people traveling to other cities. The area was newly built, and that's where the Gestapo chose to house their offices.

On 10 Av (July 24, 1942), the children's *aktion* took place.

During this *aktion*, mostly children were murdered, as were the sick and the elderly. The Germans mercilessly grabbed children from their mothers' arms and murdered them in cold blood.

Cholerina

One morning, I tried to lift my head from the pillow, but it fell back.

"Am I sick?!" I wondered. "Now? Who can allow himself to be sick in such times?!" I admonished myself in the haze.

It was the end of Elul 5702/1942. My fever rose drastically and I suffered terrible diarrhea. There was an expert doctor who lived in the building; he was of rabbinic descent and was friendly with our family. He agreed to come and treat me at no cost. After examining me he diagnosed that I was sick with a very difficult illness that was hard to cure in such times.

"What is the disease?" my mother asked tremulously.

"It's similar to cholera. More accurately, it's called cholerina," the doctor said and gathered his things. Seeing how worried Mama was, he encouraged and guided her. "Don't pay attention right now to your daughter's state of health. Just try to obtain for her a bit of healthy food so her body can get stronger, fight the disease, and overcome it."

My devoted mother ran to the neighbors and asked for their help. She went to elderly Leicha Weissman and said, "Maybe your Chaim can get some food for my Bluma'le, who is so sick?"

Chaim Weissman, thanks to his connections with the Gestapo, was able to obtain half a cup of sweet cream, which provided strength and helped heal. I drank it, and indeed, I got well…

It was a tremendous miracle. The doctor's idea—healing a cholerina patient with raging fever with a bit of healthy drink— was most strange. But that's what he claimed: under such conditions, we couldn't think of the severity of the disease, just to try and strengthen the body.

His explanation turned out to be correct, and *baruch Hashem*, I survived.

"Don't ask," one of my friends said when I went back to work. "The Germans are planning another *aktion* and ordered all the Jewish workers to hand in their ID cards."

Before the new orders, Jews and gentiles carried green ID cards. Now, ahead of the next *aktion*, the Germans ordered the Jews to change the color of their ID cards, so if a Jew tried to escape, he would be identified right away.

"What should I do?" I fretted. "They will shoot me or hang me, I didn't give in my card to change!"

My friend looked at me with pity. *There's no one to talk to,* we both thought.

Meanwhile, the rest of the Jews in the ghetto were also ordered to give in their ID cards. We were told they were being sent to the Judenrat ahead of the *aktion*. The sewing workshop workers were told that we were not part of the *aktion* because they needed our work.

When I was asked for my ID card, I gave it over fearfully. It was green, but miraculously, nothing happened to me!

They didn't give us back our ID cards. We tried to find out what happened to them and were told, "Your cards are stuck in the Judenrat!"

8

IN DARK ALLEYS

On 28 Elul 5702 (September 10, 1942), the third aktion in
Tarnow began. It lasted three days. The Nazis gathered the
Jews and kept them in one place, under the open skies, until
the aktion finished on the first day of Rosh Hashanah. Then
they transported them to their deaths.

Erev Rosh Hashanah, 5703.

W ho could think of red apples, pomegranates, and
fish heads? I myself was trembling like a fish. I
gazed in horror at the new placards that had been
hung all over town. This was the deportation order, and it said,
among other things that "Anyone who has a document signed by
the Gestapo will be able to stay in the ghetto and not go to the
assembly area."

I was trembling with fear, as I had no such document and could
not save myself. Like the other workers in the sewing workshop, I

had handed in my ID card and it was stuck at the Judenrat!

Rumors circulated around the ghetto that ten percent of the ID cards that were "stuck" were already stamped, but the clerks had not yet managed to send them to their owners.

Night fell, and with it, darkness. Tomorrow the terrible *aktion* would begin.

That night, a terrible hue and cry spread through the Tarnow ghetto; a collective wail rose from the Jewish homes. The ghetto residents sought hiding places in attics or cellars. People were petrified of the bitter fate that awaited them. Although they did not yet know of the mass murders, one thing was clear: no one came back from any of the transports.

My father, *Hy"d*, remained levelheaded even during those moments. He turned to us, his precious family and said, "I have learned from Yaakov Avinu that we must split up. We don't know what will happen to every one of us. Perhaps they will find one bunker but will not discover another place. Therefore, let us split up, like we did for the last *aktion*."

And that's how we separated forever.

My righteous, dear, pious father. My precious brothers, the scholars… They went to the attic in our small building. Mama and my sisters went to another attic.

I was the only one who didn't hide. After all, I had to go to work the following day, and for now, I was safe.

Some seventy people packed into the attic crawlspace where my mother and sisters were hiding, including little children. Accessing the entrance was complicated and entailed getting in from three different rooms. Old furniture that was no longer used was stacked in front of the doorway. The furniture belonged to the Jews who had lived there and been deported on the earlier *aktion*, never to return. The furniture was supposed to block armed intruders…

I was left alone in the house on a dark street. Chaos reigned, and people walked around blindly. I heard Jews saying to one another; "Come, let's run to the Judenrat; maybe we'll find our ID cards and see that they are stamped by the Gestapo!"

I also ran to the Judenrat office in the community building. Jewish guards stood outside, but the crowds trying to get in overwhelmed them and pushed themselves inside forcefully. I also pushed myself in. We walked through the offices until we discovered a treasure in one of the rooms—a huge stack of ID cards.

I stared at the pile, and suddenly, I saw something green peeking out in the pile!

Green—that was my color! They hadn't changed my ID card!

I had hardly managed to grasp that I could see my ID card when another lady grabbed it and looked at it. "Excuse me," I said to her. "Please show me that card!"

I gazed at the picture and saw that it was of me. It was indeed my card, stamped by the Gestapo!

The lady gave me the card and at that moment I felt as though this was my personal redemption. Now I could stay in the ghetto!

I decided to take further action.

There must be cards belonging to my friends and acquaintances in this pile, I thought to myself. *The night is long, and I can manage to save people this way!*

I searched through the huge stack until I came across a familiar name. Manya Levy! Hers was stamped. I put it in my pocket and emerged into the dark, confused street. I walked, with my emotions roiling in my heart. Ribbono shel Olam, *why did I undertake this responsibility?! I just put an entire life in my pocket! How am I supposed to know where Manya Levy lives in this ghetto?*

It was dark all around me. People walked around with small portable lamps, but who would illuminate the path for me to Manya Levy's house?

And then I had a simple idea… I would walk in the streets and call, "Who knows Manya Levy? Who knows Manya Levy?"

And that's what I did. I walked and called, in Polish and Yiddish, over and over again.

Suddenly a cry came from the darkness. "I'm her brother!"

I was overjoyed, but I wanted to be sure that the speaker was saying the truth. "Let's see, who is speaking?" I asked.

The man lit a torch and I could see his ID card with the name Levy.

What *Hashgachah pratis!* I gave him the ID card and calmed down. But I still was unable to go home on this frenetic night.

I thought of Roch'ke…

Roch'ke, the friend who I loved with all my heart. How would I be able to sit placidly, when Roch'ke's fate was crystal clear to me? I would go to her. I knew where she lived! I would go despite the fear and darkness, and I would bring her to the attic where Mama was hiding. I would ask her family to come and hide in our attic crawlspace. I wanted desperately to save them!

I loved Roch'ke and I could not come to terms with the thought that she would not be spared this terrible *aktion* and would be taken to a certain death. I went to their apartment in the ghetto. Her parents, sisters, and the little children sat there, waiting in resignation for their fate.

"Come with me, please! I came to take you to our attic. I'm begging you, listen to me and come with me! There's room there. Don't sit here and wait until they come and take you to your deaths…"

Despite my pleas, they were not convinced. "Where can we go in the middle of the night with little children?" the tired parents asked me wearily. "We will stay here. Nothing will happen to us."

I burst into tears. "Roch'ke, are you also going to stay here?" I asked bitterly.

"No, Rochele, you won't stay here," her father declared. "Go. You are stronger than we are. Go and save your life."

He pulled out several thousand dollars from a hiding place and handed them to his daughter. "This is your dowry," the poor, wretched father said. "Take it and go, my Rochele..."

I walked with her back to our attic. I pushed her inside, and moved the furniture back into place.

A Matter of Life and Death

Morning dawned.

A dark, dreadful morning.

I sat near the window and saw how people were being led away. Among the first to pass were Roch'ke's parents, sisters, and brothers, both younger and older...

My heart tore to pieces. How I had pleaded with them! How I had begged them to try to save their lives! But they had no more strength. Now they were going to be killed...

We all knew already that it was death. We didn't want to digest it, but the knowledge was clear. No one had come back alive from wherever they'd sent the people during previous *aktions*.

On the first day of the *aktion* I remained at home. Before my tearful eyes I witnessed the worst of all: my father and dear brothers were being led away... I gazed in disbelief. I parted from them from afar, tears flowing down my cheeks.

(I observed their *yahrtzeit* on 4 Tishrei. They were taken on 1 Tishrei, and it seems that all the deportees were killed three days later.)

They did not discover the attic where my mother and sisters were hiding. She and my sisters remained alive for the time being.

The beasts ran all over with huge sniffer dogs trained to detect the scent of humans. The barking was chilling; the scent of humans was everywhere. The fear of death hovered over the whole scene. Children cried, dogs barked and people wailed…

They took everyone to an assembly area, where several dozen Germans sat at long tables. The tables were full of bottles of alcoholic beverages, and the evildoers drank their fill. Their faces were red from the lust for blood and their murderous fury.

Meanwhile, other Germans went through the homes and called, "Jews, come out from wherever you are hiding. Nothing bad will happen to you!"

That's how they tricked the old and the young, small innocent children, into coming out. Many of the people preferred to believe the Germans, out of a desire to survive. And they emerged, dragging their little children behind them.

Within the hiding places, human tragedies also took place. The little children cried and the people in hiding cringed in fear. Parents were forced by the others to give their little children sleeping potions. "We won't put ourselves in danger because of a one-month-old baby. Sixty people can't die because of one baby."

And who was to know who was right, the parents of the babies or their fellow hideaways? Who could rule on matters of life and death during such mad times?!

Parents didn't know what to do with their children, young and old, and in the background, they heard the calls, "Jews, everyone, all of you, come out. Everyone should come to the assembly area. Nothing will happen to you…"

9

A Shofar...and an Akeidah

osh Hashanah 5703/1942 was the worst day of my life.
On that day, thousands of Jews were sent to their deaths,
and I was almost among them.

The sewing workshop was enveloped in a sense of calm;
we were told we would be "protected" as we were working for
the Reich. It was not true. The Germans ordered the workers
to report to the assembly area with the rest of Tarnow's Jews.
Even Jews who had recently come from ghettos in surrounding
areas joined us.

The entire area was packed with Jews. We were ordered to
sit on our knees, like prisoners. Every so often, another group
of Jews were brought in, accompanied by sniffer dogs, which
discovered bunker after bunker.

My heart trembled inside me; perhaps they had discovered
the hiding place where my mother and sisters were. I dreaded
the moment I would see them dragged over here.

Ribbono shel Olam, I prayed silently, *my father and brothers were already taken on the first day of the* aktion. *Is the fate of my dear mother and sisters also sealed? Is there something I can do? What should I be doing now?* With these torturous thoughts, I sat wrapped in myself, pleading with Hashem to have mercy...

"The quota has not yet been filled," I heard the Germans speaking among themselves. "We'll send every tenth one aside."

They sat at the long tables and sealed peoples' fates. The "selected ones" were ordered to kneel with their faces to the ground. They did so, gripping in their hands the ID cards with the coveted stamp, but at that moment, garlic peels were worth more than that stamp.

One Jew kneeled with his son beside him. The German wanted to take the son away, but the father refused. With rare courage, the man argued with the German and even slapped him across the face. The German shot him on the spot. Seeing a Yid slap a German in the face the last moment of his life offered us some consolation. It gave a bit of encouragement to those who witnessed the scene.

I noticed that the wife of our neighbor, Chaim Weissman, together with her son, were being brought to the site. The women and children were taken in carts directly to the Jewish cemetery, where they were shot.

Raizel stood in front of me; she was the tenth. My heart skipped a beat when her turn came and...she was sent to the side. But with great miracles, Raizel managed to slip back into the ranks.

And so we sat, kneeling and hunched over, as the Germans sealed our fate: this one to life; this one to death.

My neighbor clutched a child in her arms while two others gripped her dress. "Please hold one of my children," she asked me.

I agreed. I took a little girl. But just before our turn came, the girl began to protest and cried, "No! I want to go to Bubby!" The grandmother took the child.

It was another miracle of my salvation. Despite the fact that I was a young girl, had I been holding the child I would have automatically been sent to death, like all the mothers and their children.

My good friend and I gaped in disbelief at the sight of children being torn from their mothers' arms. These were the most chilling situations, of mothers who pretended to ignore their children and tossed them aside so they could stay alive. The innate, powerful will to live that courses through every human overcame every other emotion inside them. After the *selektion*, we remained standing alone in the large plaza. There were only a few of us left, and we were dejected and devastated. We looked at the piles of children's shoes, small socks, books; everything was bloodstained. Rivers of blood flowed from the children and their mothers, who had been shot by those bestial monsters.

Anyone who didn't experience that bloodbath cannot understand the depths of the abyss. It was worse than the worst possible thing we could have imagined, literally the valley of death. It was the most appalling *selektion* I ever experienced.

There were difficult things later on as well. I went through camps and experienced true Gehinnom. But those horrific scenes remain etched in my memory, images of piles of shoes and clothes of babies, children, and toddlers, stained with their blood, mixed with their mothers' blood—those were the worst images I ever saw in my life.

Eretz, al techasi damam!

May Our Shofar Blasts Rise

The *selektion* continued for three days straight, during which ten thousand Jews were murdered; children were tortured and tossed into the river; they were shot or rolled down slopes together with their mothers.

Towards sunset, the Germans led away all those who had been sent aside and had been kneeling, but had not yet been shot. They were taken to an unknown location, and after some time, we learned that they had been murdered in a most horrific way. Eight thousand Jews were sent from that *aktion* to the Belzec death camp, including my father and my brothers, the pure and holy Mordechai and Moshe Yehoshua, *Hy"d*.

We returned home shattered and shaken. En route, my brother-in-law, Avrume'le raised his eyes Heavenwards. The sun was still casting yellow-reddish rays; it was the final moments before sunset.

"We can still fulfill the mitzvah of *tekias shofar* on time," his parched lips murmured.

We reached the house. Avrume'le took the shofar in hand, closed his eyes, made the *brachah*, and blew. We fulfilled the mitzvah. The shofar blasts, the *tekiah, shevarim,* and *teruah*, rose up from the bleeding ghetto on those final moments of Rosh Hashanah 5703. *Tekias shofar* drowning in blood that surely penetrated all the Heavenly firmaments.

The next day, I saw Chaim, my neighbor, waiting to get in to the Gestapo. He thought perhaps in the merit of his connections he could do something for his wife and child. Poor man, he thought they were still alive. I had no way to tell him that, tragically, I had seen them shot.

After the *selektion*, a deathly silence fell on the ghetto.

Everything was enveloped in sadness, emptiness, and the silence was more deafening than all the screaming and wailing that had preceded it. The apartments were empty. Entire families, or large parts of them, had been mercilessly wiped out.

Concurrently, I began to receive some news about my father. Someone told us that he had seen him, and that we should send him a tallis, tefillin, and a sweater. They had apparently seen someone who resembled my father.

When we heard this, we tried to console ourselves and live with the illusion that the Germans had taken the people to work, and that we would yet meet up with our loved ones in the future.

In reality, not a trace remained of the deportees of the Tarnow ghetto *selektions*.

Yankel sat at the table, his skinny hands trembling as he fed himself spoon after spoon of soup.

Yankel was a *bochur* who had come to our apartment in the ghetto with his aunt from the Sanzer ghetto. The ghetto had been liquidated and the survivors had been sent to Tarnow. They did the same with other ghettos, and began to fill the Tarnow ghetto again. The Germans treated Jews like sardines packed into a can, and those living in the ghetto had to open the already crowded apartments to the new arrivals.

My mother preferred to think that my father and brothers were alive and working somewhere. She gave Yankel and his aunt some of our food, telling Yankel with fervent hope: "In the merit of my serving you soup, I hope that someone is having mercy on my Mordche'le and giving him a plate of soup wherever he is…"

10

RIVKA'LE HOLDS HER BREATH

E ven after the dreadful *selektion* of Rosh Hashanah 5703,
I continued working at the sewing workshop. My sister
Sarah Baila began to work paving roads.

At the beginning of Cheshvan 5703/October 1942, our ghetto
was divided in two by a fence. Ghetto A was like a "dormitory"
for workers, with separate areas for men and women. The
commander of the ghetto was Blacher. Ghetto B was where Jews
who did not work and large families lived. The commander
there was Grunoff. In every *aktion* from then on, they took Jews
from Ghetto B.

Once the ghetto was divided, I no longer slept in the same
place as my mother and sisters. As I worked in the sewing
workshop, I had to live with the workers in Ghetto A, while my
mother and sisters lived in Ghetto B. Despite it being forbidden,
I occasionally crossed over to visit my loved ones.

The separation from my family was one of the most difficult

chapters of the Holocaust for me. As long as I was with my family, I had the strength to endure the travails. After we were separated, I was heartbroken.

4 Cheshvan 5703 (October 15, 1942)

Snow accumulated on the roads and covered the rooftops with a white blanket. I looked out of the window of the sewing workshop, from where I had a view of the ghetto.

"Oh, no!" I gasped. To my horror, I saw many military vehicles surrounding the ghetto. That could only mean one thing: another *selektion!*

I wasn't wrong. Another deportation, another one of the horrible *selektions.*

Three thousand people were sent to an unknown destination; the *selektion* was also replete with torture and murders. My dear sister Sarah Baila, *Hy"d*, was taken with all the other people who worked paving roads. I have no idea where they took her or what she experienced until she breathed her last. No one ever returned alive from the deportations; my sister was no different. Later we learned that they had all been taken to die at Belzec.

My brother-in-law Avrume'le, Raizel's husband, decided to find a good hiding place where they could take cover during *selektions.* He discovered a door beneath the stairs at the top of our building, which led to a tiny storage room that could hold two people at most.

That tiny room was the miracle of the salvation of my dear family!

While I was looking worriedly out the window of the sewing workshop, my mother was standing at the window of her house, looking towards the plaza where the *selektions* were usually conducted. She saw that the Germans were starting to encircle the ghetto. They burst inside and with feral brutality, broke into homes, grabbed people, and sent them to the plaza.

Mama became terribly frightened, and was about to go out to the balcony of the building, from where she would take cover in the attic, as she had done during previous *selektions*. But suddenly, she saw the image of her father in her mind; he was no longer among the living. He stood before her in all his glory, as though he was alive, and seemed to grasp her hand and call to her, "*Esther, no! I do not allow you to go up to the attic to hide under any circumstances!*"

She froze, thunderstruck. Meanwhile, the Germans were coming closer to the house. And then, in a flash, she fled via the large balcony to the tiny storage room where Raizel and her husband were hiding.

My sisters Chaya, Necha, and Rivka'le ran after her. And this is where a miracle took place: the place could not really hold more than two people, but somehow, five squeezed in: Mama, Raizel and her husband, Chaya, and Necha.

My grandfather accompanied his daughter, my mother, and protected her from his place On High. It turned out that the attic where Mama had planned to hide was discovered by the Nazis, and everyone hiding there was taken away!

For now, Mama had been saved.

Little Rivka'le was the last one to run after Mama and the girls, but she was too late. A German soldier who entered the building noticed her.

Rivka'le saw that the German had caught sight of her, so she ran back inside.

The house was empty. I was at work, and the others were hiding. Time was short and the German was coming up the stairs…

At the last second, Rivka'le dove onto a bed and hid beneath the piles of blankets and linens.

The German burst into the house and began to scream wildly: "Where is the little blonde girl with the braids? Where did she run?"

He was shrieking furiously, and his bloodthirsty friends entered the house after him. They ran all over, holding their weapons, searching in every corner. They reached the bed where Rivka'le was laying, and she felt the cold butt of the gun poking her body but they didn't realize she was there. She held her breath, terrified that if the blanket would move with her breaths, they would see her. The soldiers were livid: "*Voh iz zi?* Where is she?"

They kept dashing around the house in a crazed frenzy, as though they were drugged, until they finally gave up and left.

Angels had been watching over Rivka'le!

That night was white and snowy, and I snuck home after the day at work. I was greeted by an empty, dark, silent home. I burst into tears and cried: "Mama! Where are you? Where is Chaya? Necha? Where is Rivka'le?"

No one heard my cries and calls.

"Rivky, Rivka'le! Are you also not here?" I wailed.

Only then did Rivka'le dare emerge from beneath the blankets and reveal herself. She was pale and trembling. "Where is Mama?" I asked fearfully.

"I think she's hiding somewhere near the stairs. I saw her and Chaya and Necha running there," Rivka said, her voice shaking. She had not yet recovered from the trauma of what she had been through. "Let's go find her," she added.

It was pitch dark in the ghetto. It was wartime, and there were blackout orders, which meant we sat in near complete darkness. We began to call out, "Mama! Necha! Chaya! Raizel!"

The people in hiding heard us and returned the calls.

"The Gestapo isn't here anymore, the Germans have gone!" we called to them.

Only then did they emerge from their hiding place, and to our great joy, we saw that we had experienced another miracle. They were still alive.

Where Are the Shoes?

On 17 Tammuz 5703, I crossed the fence that bisected the ghetto to the part where my mother was; I was carrying a pair of shoes. They were torn here and there, but they were still usable. I joined Mama for a meal after the fast. We spoke, and infused each other with strength. Then I asked her, "Mama, please give my shoes to the shoemaker so he can repair them."

Mama did it for me, and after the repair she returned the shoes to me. That evening, I returned as usual to the sewing workshop, and lay down to sleep. When I awoke in the morning I recoiled: My shoes were gone! I had put them on the night table right near my bed! I was one hundred percent sure of it! My eyes searched all around me, but for naught; the shoes were gone!

Dejectedly, I went over to the supervisor and told him my shoes had been stolen.

Shoes were worth a fortune at the time, probably more than $1,000 in today's money. I didn't have the money to obtain new shoes.

"Go to the Jewish judges, they will help you," the supervisor said.

I refused. I didn't want to report Jewish women, even though I definitely suspected them. I didn't trust the workers who spoke and acted in such a lowly fashion.

"Did you see with your own eyes how they stole your shoes?" I asked myself. The answer was "no!" Therefore, I refrained from reporting it. I mourned my lost shoes, while the women around me laughed off my dejection.

It was very disheartening for me to have to spend my time among such people, who could take things that were not theirs. I felt horrible over the fact that I was associating with thieves.

A short time passed. One very rainy, stormy day, as I sat and sewed, the women around me talked about the seasonal flooding of the ghetto.

My mother and sisters lived on the top floor in the ghetto, over the *bais medrash* of the Rav of Zhabna, so they didn't suffer from the rain. But many other families lived on the ground floor, and the rain flooded their homes. Several of my workmates visited their own flooded homes, and suddenly—surprise! In one of their homes, floating on the water, they encountered no more and no less…my shoes!

"Bluma, look what we found!" They presented me with the shoes.

I was overjoyed and surprised. And then I remembered!

When I had returned from visiting Mama after my shoes were repaired, I passed between the two ghettos, as I always did. When I entered the house on the border, I must have put my shoes down on the windowsill. The window was hewn into the deep stone, similar to those in Yerushalmi stone homes.

The shoes stood there waiting for days, and no one took them. In the morning, people hurried to work, and at night, they hardly managed to eat something before they fell into bed, exhausted. There was no time to search for valuable findings.

And I had been so sure that I had been robbed…

For me, it was a lifelong lesson. I learned an important principle: don't suspect anyone of something you did not see them do with your own eyes. Even if you are one hundred percent sure that they did something wrong, there are times it is impossible to know what really happened. Often, the mistake becomes clear after some time, and all the questions are clarified.

At that moment, the words of *Chazal* became so real for me: "Judge every person favorably" (*Avos*, 1, 6).

"Eat and drink for tomorrow you may die," says the Navi (*Yeshayahu* 22, 13). This is a chilling prophecy which came true in the ghetto between one deportation and the next.

Sometimes, it was possible to smuggle some ersatz whiskey that had been self-produced into the ghetto. The real whiskey was very expensive and unobtainable. Some of the ghetto residents drank and became drunk as a way to escape their plight. They could live without seeing the horrific reality unfolding around them.

Marriages took place without any thought for the future…life had become a dazed and numbing confusion.

Just Not in a Convent

Nine more months of 5703 passed in fear and constant tension of what was in store, until Elul 5703/1943. During this time, there were occasional small *selektions*; on 3 Elul, the mass *selektion* that liquidated the ghetto completely and decimated the rest of its Jews took place.

Meanwhile, we tried to smuggle little Rivka'le to safety.

One morning, Mama carefully braided her blonde braids, and dressed her in villager's clothes, as she whispered tearful words of parting.

Rivka'le set out to our aunt, who lived in a village near Krakow. Aunt Chaya was living under an assumed identity with fake ID papers. She had gentile acquaintances, and they fed her a steady supply of news from the Tarnow ghetto. At the end of each *selektion*, my aunt sent them to find out who of us had survived and who was going to work. The gentile also brought us the bit of foodstuffs that our aunt sent.

Now, we were able to smuggle Rivka'le out of the ghetto in an ingenious way; my aunt had sent a gentile to wait for her. He took Rivka'le to her house.

Rivka'le's blonde braids made her look Aryan. She looked like a born and bred Polish country girl, but the people who lived nearby and did not know her began to get suspicious. They were wary of the new face that had arrived in the village.

After a few weeks they began to harass Rivka'le with probing questions: "Who are you, little girl?" "What are you doing here?" "Why did you come?"

She heard them telling each other in a knowing tone, with hostile expressions, "Ahhh, she must be one of the Jews!"

Our aunt began to fret. "Things are getting too hot around Rivka'le. Her life is in danger. What should I do?"

A gentile acquaintance gave her some advice. "The best thing to do is to send the girl to a convent, so they won't interrogate her anymore and won't suspect her of being a Jewess."

Aunt Chaya recoiled at the very idea. She knew that my pious mother would be very distraught if her daughter was placed in a convent.

Many Jewish children were lost to convents during the war. Live parts of the Jewish nation were cut off in the shadow of Christianity, because their parents wanted to save them from death. To this day, many of them and their descendants do not even know they are Jewish.

Rivka'le was no longer a little child; she well remembered what she had absorbed in her parents' home. Nevertheless, my aunt did not dare send her to a convent without asking my mother. She sent a messenger to get permission from Mama, but my mother adamantly refused. Her answer was unequivocal: "Absolutely not!"

It was the *mesirus nefesh* of a loving mother who preferred the spiritual life of her dear Rivka'le to the empty life of a non-Jew cut off from her nation. Although the sword hovered over their heads, and there was a chance to save her life in the convent— Mama chose a life of eternity for her daughter.

Rivka'le was sent back to the Tarnow ghetto.

Reentering the ghetto was very risky. Many people were shot trying to sneak their way in. Sometimes, a local gentile noticed Jews trying to get in and informed on them to the Gestapo.

Despite the danger, wise little Rivka'le managed to smuggle herself back into the ghetto the same way she was smuggled out. This time, too, she had tremendous *siyata diShmaya*, and she reached us safely.

How we all rejoiced when she returned! We were so thrilled to have our darling Rivka'le back! But her return also meant the end of any chance to stay alive. Had she remained with our aunt, perhaps she would have survived.

That's what *Hashgachah* ordained, so that's what had to happen...[1]

---

1. The family notes: Rivka'le's image always hovered in our home. We heard a lot about her. Our mother was most distraught over her loss and tortured herself with thoughts of perhaps and maybe…Rivka'le could have hidden in our aunt's house and survived, and be alive to this day.

11

MOTHER SENT ME TO LIVE

I woke up on 2 Elul 5703/1943 to a cacophony of screaming and wailing from the surrounding homes. I hurried to the window, along with my fellow workers, and looked out to see large numbers of soldiers surrounding the entire ghetto. The final *selektion*, the one we had been dreading for so long, had begun!

My entire body began to tremble. I had no idea what to do! Should I remain in the sewing workshop? Should I go to Mama? No place was safe anymore! I tried to think rationally despite my frightened state. Finally, I decided: I would run to the other ghetto to be with my mother and sisters. What was my life worth if I survived by myself? What would I gain by remaining alive while they were taken from me? Life alone was not worth it for me. I wanted to be with my family!

These thoughts galvanized me into a mad dash for the other ghetto.

I ran and ran, and suddenly noticed my dear mother and

sisters running towards me. They also wanted to reunite with me. During those pivotal moments, we wanted to be together...

We continued running to where Raizel lived in Ghetto B. When we arrived at the house, Raizel and her husband urged us to hurry. "Quick! Let's get into our little attic hiding place!"

We all darted up the stairs. I wanted to join them, but then Mama stopped me. She called to me emotionally, "Bluma, no...*I want something to remain of our family!* Go back to work. You have a chance to live!"

Those were crucial, fateful moments—the moments in which I was sent to life.

At that very minute, the evil beast, Amon Goeth, *ym"s*, notorious for his brutality, burst into the building. He looked like a monster. "What are you standing there for? Go home and bring clothes and linens!" he thundered. He took special enjoyment in watching Jewish women dragging the bundles that would be useless to them.

Mama pressed 200 zlotys into my hand. It was almost all she had to her name. "Maybe you'll be able to get food to bring to us," she said, and we parted.

I ran frantically back to the sewing workshop, but I quickly found out that our fate was also dire. The gates were locked, like the rest of the factories in the ghetto that had been closed to Jews. They no longer needed our work. The Jews of Tarnow were finally being sent to their bitter end.

We quickly packed up clothes, linens, and other items. Later, we were ordered to abandon everything and not to take a thing. The Germans marched us out of the ghetto, walking on either side of us and shooting indiscriminately, so that no one would dare step out of line.

The scenes at the assembly plaza were appalling. Mothers had wrapped their most valuable treasures—their little children who were somehow still alive—in their linens. Babies and children up to the age of four were concealed in the covers, and, carrying these heavy loads on their shoulders, the mothers stood in the plaza all night long.

Among the people there, I noticed my cousin, a *bochur* who had been caught up in the winds of those times but who was saved by Belzer *chassidim* who managed to bring him back and turn him into a devoted Belzer *chassid*. He was known for his brilliance and *Yiras Shamayim*. In the ghetto, he did not use dairy products because they did not have the most *mehudar hechsher*. He didn't want to drink milk or use butter that was not *chalav Yisrael*.

This pious *bochur* did not touch his beard throughout the war, and his face was always wrapped in a scarf to conceal it. The Nazis were liable to kill him for this "sin" but he was not deterred. With an aching heart, I watched them drag him, thin and scrawny as a stick, out of the rows of people. They chose him to be their sacrifice, sending him to the unknown.

The Jews stood in the large plaza all night. We had to watch the Nazis pour benzene onto the buildings and set them aflame, so that anyone hiding inside would be forced out. The scene was excruciatingly painful.

The Death Wagon

The local Poles were only too pleased at what was happening. They were not allowed to leave their homes the day of the *selektion*, so that there would be no witnesses to the crimes. Perhaps one out of ten thousand had pity on us, not more.

We reached the train station, where we were ordered to throw all of our possessions into a wagon. At that moment, a terrible hue and cry rose from the crowd. I could not look at the mothers who were carrying their children in their bundles. They cried and screamed and refused to throw their live baggage and leave it unsupervised. They could not part from their precious children, who they had protected with such *mesirus nefesh* until that point.

The children also wailed. I gazed in horror and helplessness at my sister's friend, who was hiding her child in a bundle clutched to her bosom and who now had to face this unbearable order.

There were those mothers who managed somehow to push their way onto the passenger car together with their precious cargo, and breathed a sigh of relief, thinking the danger had passed for now…

The train stood in its place. The Germans announced in German, Polish, and Yiddish that if a single child would be found in the car, they would shoot all its occupants. Again, a tumult swirled inside the car: those inside urged the woman that had been able to get in with the child, "Go out with your child. We don't want to die because of you!"

A twelve-year-old child succeeded in mingling in with the adults. The Jewish supervisor, who searched the crowds for children who were hiding and dragged them outside, did not notice him. Later, a German did another inspection and caught the child. The father pleaded desperately for his child's life, but to no avail. The father and son were murdered inside the train car. All the children whose parents tried to save them met a similar end, *Hashem Yikom Damam*!

We were not allowed to take anything with us, not even a spoon. The Germans were afraid we would be able to use a spoon to force open the little window in the car, and see what was happening outside and perhaps even escape. They searched all our pockets and announced that anyone who would be found holding something would be shot. We were very frightened and handed over everything we had. The car that we were loaded onto was intended to transport cattle.

We were packed in, crushed really, and we could barely stand or even sit on the stairs. After a long wait, and many more deaths, the train began to move. Darkness fell; we had no water and were in the most inhuman conditions.

Tarnow—The End

Meanwhile, what was happening to my mother and sisters?

When I went with my co-workers to the assembly area, my mother, Raizel and her husband, Necha Breindel, Chaya, and Rivka'le remained in the ghetto, hiding in the attic of Raizel and Avrume'le's building.

My family hid in the attic for three weeks. Like the rest of the survivors who hid in the ghetto, they suffered terrible starvation and thirst. At night, when it was dark they took their lives in their hands, slipped out, and ran to abandoned apartments to search for food that people may have left behind. They also rummaged through the garbage to find leftovers and peels to save themselves from dying of hunger.

Ultimately, they also met their bitter end.

A German gentile named Placher lived in the ghetto. Until the war, he had been known for his good relationship with the Jews. He went from apartment to apartment calling: "Everyone out! Nothing will happen to you! You will live! Don't worry! Come on out!"

There were those who believed him. The terrible hunger flushed people out of their hiding places. They preferred to live with illusions and believe the deceitful Placher, and crawled out from attics. My mother, sisters, and brother-in-law did the same. By contrast, there were those who did not emerge and they remained alive.

All those who came out of their hiding places were loaded into a vehicle that took them to the Tchebna camp, not far from the Polish Hungarian border.

From the first moment, they were forced to work extremely hard, and their condition deteriorated over time. Anyone who had money was sometimes able to buy things from the Germans. After some time, they were transferred to the Hungarian border where they were shot to death, leaving not a trace of their existence.

Seven hundred Jews perished with my mother and sisters in Tchebna. These figures appear in the book that commemorates the murder in Tchebna on that date. *Hashem Yikom Damam.*

I received the information from a *bochur*, a refugee from the Sanzer ghetto who lived in our house in the Tarnow ghetto. The *bochur* remained alive because he had a skill that was valued by the Germans. After the war, he came to the kibbutz of survivors in Krakow and saw my name on the list of people seeking information about my family. He sent me a letter detailing the fate of my mother and sisters, and the rest of the Tarnow ghetto.

The *bochur* saw my mother, sisters, and brother-in-law killed. May their pure, innocent, refined souls rest in eternal peace.

Tarnow, my beautiful city, which had pulsed with Jewish and chassidic life until it was destroyed, remained bereft of Jews. Only a tiny group of Jews were left, charged with cleaning the ghetto and organizing the possessions of the deportees. Of the rest, 7,000 people were sent to Birkenau and 3,000 people were sent to Plashow.

I was among the latter, taken to Plashow, where a new chapter in my life began.

12

WELCOME TO PLASHOW

A fter traveling for two hours in the cattle car, we reached Krakow. We stopped only for a short time, because Jews were "forbidden" to spend time in the city.

In order to humiliate the Polish culture and tradition, the Germans declared Krakow, and not Warsaw, to be the capital of Poland. As a result, the governor, Frank, ym"s, who Hitler appointed, forbid the "inferior" Jews from being in the city. Therefore, all the Jews of Krakow were transferred to nearby Plashow.

In Krakow I met acquaintances from Bais Yaakov who had worked with me in the sewing workshop. Together, we continued to Plashow, located not far from Krakow.

We entered the gates of Plashow and were immediately assailed by deafening loudspeakers: "No hiding money! Anyone who has any money at all—throw it out!"

Again and again, and again...it's forbidden to have money or any other valuables... The ban was so rigid that the Germans were liable to kill someone if they found a tiny zloty coin on him.

What a welcome we had from the Germans, *ym"s*.

That was hardly all! We were also in for an especially traumatic welcome from our Jewish brethren. We were horrified to hear harsh, humiliating, vulgar language from the Jewish commandos who addressed us. They beat us and treated us horribly. It was obvious that they were already veterans at the camp, and that the suffering and tribulations they had been through had sapped every last drop of humanity out of them. That was the objective of the Germans—to destroy the humanness!

We were "new" and still recoiled from the beatings and humiliation that poured forth from our fellow Jews. We were also weak and hungry, and what did we get? A portion of some type of fatty food that revulsed us.

And then I heard Mrs. Rivka Pinkusewicz, who was a teacher in Bais Yaakov before the war, whisper, "Yidden, don't eat. The food is treif!"

Mrs. Pinkusewicz had previously been in the Krakow ghetto, along with many other G-d fearing Yidden. Some of them had worked in the kitchen and were able to keep three pots kosher by preventing meat from being put into them. "Meat" was really only bones that didn't even add a good flavor, but they were enough to make the pots *treif*.

Indeed, those righteous people from Krakow were spared from eating treif food. Often the Germans made a point of tossing treif bones into the kosher pots, so that those keeping kosher wouldn't have what to eat. When that happened, some of the Yidden gave up on the soup and sufficed only on the bread.

Mrs. Pinkusewicz thought that in Plashow, too, it would be possible to keep a pot kosher, but regretfully, there were no such luxuries there. According to *halachah*, we were allowed to eat, because our lives were in danger.

The Plashow camp was built on two Jewish cemeteries. We had to walk on the graves, and we felt awful about it. We tried to avoid desecrating graves as best we could; we would pick up pieces from the headstones to clear ourselves a path to walk.

We were treated worse than slaves, and spoken to in such a humiliating way that it depressed us and grated on our ears.

The biggest challenge for me during that time was being cut off from my family. It was so painful to be apart from them. How I missed them, my dear, kind mother and my darling sisters. "We'll tie ourselves together so they can't separate us," I recalled the words we had pledged to each other at the beginning of the war. Hah! How innocent we had been, what a sweet, unrealistic dream....And meanwhile, the brutal reality was hitting me in the face...

Still, I was able to find a familiar face here and there, which lifted my spirits somewhat.

The "beds" that waited for us in the camp were just planks, stacked several tiers high. Every day, we got a slice of bread and a little pot of soup. We weren't given plates or spoons. We had to drink directly from the pot. One day, youths from the camp gave us slats of wood that they had sharpened, which served as a sort of "spoon" for us.

The hunger wreaked havoc on the prisoners. People sold themselves for one spoon of soup. It wasn't unusual to see a starving mother push her daughter out of the way to get a spoon of soup for herself, or the daughter pushing the mother...

This humiliation was the pinnacle of triumph for the Nazis, exactly what they aspired to do! They wanted to dehumanize and degrade the noble Jewish nation, known for its refined character traits, to bring it to such a low point, to kill the body and torture the soul...

A few of us were able to smuggle in some money, at great personal risk, and in exchange, we purchased some food. Those who had money sent it with the groups that went to work at a far-off location outside of the camp, and they bought food for them.

The Candies

Rosa was a young woman who had been expelled from Germany to Poland. She had managed to save a few dollars from her dowry. Every time she went to work outside the camp, she chose to purchase...candies! It was easy to smuggle them into the camp, and their sweetness revived her a bit.

Rosa was extremely kind. She didn't eat the candies herself, but rather, she shared them. Each day, she gave a candy to one friend, and that was a lot!

I remember when my turn came how I sucked the candy slowly, carefully, like a man sipping from life-giving water. I keenly felt the sweetness reviving me, infusing my every limb with some strength.

Until the war, I had no predilection for sweets. I didn't drink sweetened coffee or tea because I saw no point to it. But in the camp, I began to crave sweets and the sense of renewal they offered.

I had already tasted the candies while working in the sewing workshop in the Tarnow ghetto. Beside me at the table worked an older woman who could have been my mother. She also liked buying candies on the sly and would share them with me, whispering longingly, "Let me imagine that I'm giving these candies to my daughter."

I let her... The woman's children had been taken from her and sent to their deaths. She herself survived the war, but unfortunately, never had more children.

On occasion, we would even see displays of kindness at the bread distribution. Normally, there were fights whenever the bread was given out. People argued and screamed that their slice was half a millimeter thinner, and that the next person had sliced a fatter slice for himself. Against this backdrop, there were also examples of exceptional generosity and kindness, which I also benefited from at various times. Those rays of *ahavas Yisrael* in the darkness fired up the hope in our hearts that Am Yisrael would survive for eternity.

We were cold…and sad…

The iciness cut into our flesh. I walked, frozen, from here to there, carrying pieces of wood on my shoulders. Then I returned the wood to the place I had taken them from.

Why did the Germans make us do such senseless work? What was the purpose?

No reason; it was just to torture me and my friends.

I hadn't been especially happy at the sewing workshop in Tarnow, but at least I was in a stone building. Here, at Plashow, we were housed in wooden barracks. The Polish cold penetrated our bones, and anyone who worked outside the barracks suffered immeasurably from the cold.

The unfulfilling work shattered my spirits. When a person works hard, even if the work is very difficult, and even if he is serving the enemy—he still has a sense of productivity. But to work and exert yourself with no purpose was terribly frustrating! Such work makes a person feel so terrible, it kills him.

That was part of the Germans' way of crushing us. They didn't let the Jews rest; if there was no work for them, their feverish minds came up with senseless, numbing tasks.

Later on, I worked producing bombs for the Germans, which

for me, was preferable. At least I didn't have that dreadful feeling of working at Pisom and Ramses, useless, senseless work, even though my new job meant I was helping the German war machine.

But apparently there was no limit to the depths of this bottomless Gehinnom...

After some time I was ordered to carry planks that were used as fodder for the fires used to burn dead bodies. The Germans would shoot Jews and toss them into a nearby pit. From afar, we would see the Jews standing, and then collapsing from the gunfire. Then they were tossed into the pit.

Our job was to carry boards, and then ignite the fire to burn the bodies...

For the Sin of Potatoes

As winter approached, the Poles would hide potatoes under mounds of earth to prevent them from freezing.

One day, while I was dragging wood on my shoulders, I saw people roasting potatoes. The smell carried from far, and caused us starving people to grow dizzy with longing.

We wanted to eat...just a bit of potato, just a bit!

We waited for the guards to leave us for a minute and ran in the direction of the aroma of roasting potatoes. We thought we'd take a few potatoes, and somehow, be able to cook them. (There were people who ate raw potatoes also.)

What a fateful mistake!

The evil guards observed us from afar as we grabbed the potatoes desperately. Each one of us stuffed two or three spuds into our pockets and...we were caught.

Obviously there was a commensurate punishment for such a severe crime!

The group of "sinners" was taken to a small jail on the outskirts of the camp. It was a very dangerous place. That was where people were taken after they were discovered hiding under Aryan identities; from there they were taken to the Gestapo headquarters in Krakow—the worst place of all, from which almost no one emerged alive.

The fiendish Lagerfuehrer (camp commander), Amon Goeth, *ym"s*, would go into the jail every day to take pleasure in watching the sadistic tortures carried out there.

We were greeted at the police station with brutal beatings. Our faces were bruised until they bled and swelled.

We wailed and cried. We pleaded for our lives. What had we done? We took a few measly potatoes... But the German didn't even listen to us and continued his whipping.

One by one we were taken to the jail. We were ordered to lay down on the planks. We had no human amenities; it was much worse than in the camp. In the camp we also slept on planks, but here, there was one plank for all of us to share, and the sanitary conditions were beyond dreadful.

Suddenly someone arrived to inform us that the Lagerfueher was about to arrive and who knows what he was going to do to us. "I'm trembling in fear," he told us.

We were deeply traumatized by what happened during the course of the evening.

A few people who had missed a day of work were taken out. They were hung on the gallows, not to die but as a form of torture, with their shoulders on the rope and their heads slack. These were extremely painful moments. We heard the crying and pleading, victims begging to be taken down already because the torture was unbearable—all to no avail. This macabre act continued for about an hour, with the poor men hanging from under their shoulders, until they were roughly taken down.

The man who came in to us continued to scare us: "Oh, the crying that came from here, the crying..."

Our fear mounted, pressing into us like a chokehold.

The night darkened, and meanwhile, nothing happened to us.

Close to midnight, a German opened the gate of the jail, hurling epithets, and walloped each of us with a truncheon. Then he sent us on our way.

We ran back to our barracks, our faces swollen from the beating—but we had been released and were overjoyed.

Woe unto such a release, into the labor camp in the valley of death. But with such proportions of evil ranging around us, we were thrilled to be able to return to our barracks and that we were spared something worse.

Our friends greeted us joyfully. "Don't ask, everyone was talking about you and we were so worried," they told us.

We were starving; we didn't get any of those potatoes, and had been fed only torture, but we had been miraculously spared and allowed to return to the land of the living.

13

IN THE STONE QUARRY

*S*ongs of hope,
stones tumbling down the slope,
frozen nights
and eyes that longed for sleep...

All these are flashes of memories from the stone quarry in Plashow.

The six weeks of terror remain forever etched in my memory. The frigid temperatures that plunged sharply below zero, the backbreaking, dangerous work, and on the other hand—how many wonderful attributes Am Yisrael displayed, even in the depths of the Gehinnom. It is to those displays of compassion and *ahavas Yisrael* that were sent to us from beyond the wall, by tortured, exhausted prisoners—that I would like to pay tribute.

Our work was the most difficult and dangerous in the Plashow camp.

A regular prisoner worked one week on the day shift and the next week on the night shift. That's how it was for most; but in the stone quarry, we worked for six straight weeks on the night shift.

A person's biological clock is not set to work at night and sleep by day. It's impossible to alter nature and make up the hours of sleep during the day in order to work at night. This kind of mix-up causes extreme exhaustion.

But that's what we were ordered to do. Our job was to pave a road near the villa of the Lagerführer, the evil Amon Goeth, *ym"s,* and we were told to do it at night.

This is how we worked: there were two rocky mountains near the camp. The prisoners were ordered to detonate explosives against the boulders and then to load the stones that broke off onto small metal carts that were connected to each other like a train. The carts were tied to large, thick ropes, whose diameter was like that of the human leg.

We would stand, seventy women in a row, and each one took a rope over her shoulder. Together, we climbed the hill, carrying the heavy load of carts weighed down by rocks. When we reached the top, we had to unload the rocks, which were used to pave the road.

Then we had to run down the mountainous hills, and again blow up part of the mountain, load up the carts, climb the mountain… This process repeated itself over and over.

Initially, gentile prisoners were tasked with this work. They blew up the rocks and loaded the stones into the carts, and an electric motor powered the little train up the mountain. After some time, the Germans asked themselves a question of cold logic: Why did the non-Jews have to work so hard? The Jews could do it!

So Jewish men were assigned to this work.

After some more time passed, the Nazis began to wonder why they needed the electric motor. They had people with a natural motor—two legs! Let them drag the carts up the mountain with their own power.

Ultimately, they came up with an even more "brilliant" evil plan: Why should men do this work? It was too easy! The women could be assigned to the task...

The overseer thought that the shifts should be arranged such that night and day shifts alternated each week. He explained to the Lagerführer that the Jewesses might collapse if they would work continuous night shifts.

"That's exactly what I want—that they should collapse!" the shameless fiend roared with laughter.

It was December and January, when Poland's winter is at its peak, and we had to work during those frozen nights. They tortured us for six excruciating weeks, which left their impression on my body for the rest of my life.

The difficulty made us go out of our minds. In general, everyone at Plashow looked out only for himself. A mother and daughter fought over a crumb of bread, but despite the general egoism, *everyone* pitied the women working in the stone quarry. We were considered to be the most wretched of all.

At six in the evening, when the prisoners returned from work, we would make our way to the quarry to begin our shift. The prisoners gazed at us and we heard them whispering, "*Nebach, nebach*, the *shtein broch* are already going to work."

And then, they began throwing various items at us...warm gloves, a scarf, or any other warm garment that the other prisoners took off themselves. It was remarkable and moving. People gave up vital items that their lives depended on—for us.

How much Jewish strength was manifested in these heroic acts! The Nazis did everything in their power to dull and crush the innate giving and mercy that our nation is blessed with; they turned the prisoners into rabidly selfish people, but despite all that, they did not succeed in robbing them of their *tzelem Elokim*. They were unable to obliterate the little scrap of soul that remained within us.

In the moment of truth, the latent compassion that lay deep within came to life, and the natural Jewish nature of giving rose to the fore…

It was true *matan b'seser*. We didn't know who the givers were. We just caught whatever they threw, whether it was a warm kerchief to wrap the head, a wooly scarf, or gloves, and warmed our bodies and souls at once.

And It Was Midnight

It was dark and cold, and we were working, exerting ourselves, hacking boulders, dragging stones, and running back and forth. We worked all night without receiving a morsel to eat or drink. But each night at midnight, the same act of *chessed* repeated itself: the slave laborers on the other side of the wall risked their lives and sent over a huge pot of hot coffee to infuse our tortured bodies and souls with a bit of life.

I will never forget those moments of revival. It was another deeply moving display of compassion in the depths of the darkness…

The Germans aspired to depress and humiliate us to the point where we were zero—in body and soul—but there, in the darkness and the cold, the noble Jewish character traits rose to the surface, and illuminated the darkness with their rays.

The Jewish kapo also displayed consideration for us. If someone asked to go out for a few minutes, and would then be gone for half an hour or an hour, he didn't scream about the delay, because he felt bad for us.

The Lagerführer who lived right nearby would spend his nights feasting and drinking. Suddenly, the window to his room would open and his evil eyes would follow us doing the quarry work. If he didn't like something he saw, he would get dressed and come out for an inspection.

"Where are all seventy?" he would howl.

There was hardly ever a time when all seventy prisoners were present, because the kapo always allowed ten or fifteen of us to take a break, ostensibly for the bathroom, if they felt very weak.

The Lagerführer would count us, and regularly, it happened that he was blinded. "Correct! *Shtimt!*" he would declare. The number was right—he had counted seventy. He never discovered someone missing.

Thus we witnessed the Divine *Hashgachah* every step of the way, even in the valley of death.

Even in Gehinnom it is possible to sing. We discovered this fact during those horrific nights.

While climbing up the mountains, we would hum a song that one of us had composed. Her sense of humor had somehow survived the inferno. With fantasies and illusions, several of the prisoners somehow managed to compose songs in that dismal place... When we reached the top of the mountain and emptied our load of rocks, the kapo allowed us to rest on the stones before we had to run back down the mountain with the carts.

We sat on the frozen rocks and all caught severe rheumatism. All the workers of the quarry who survived received this "gift" as an eternal memento.

But the most dreadful part of the work was when there was a backwards slide.

It would happen when one of the women in the row eased her grip a bit, and the entire row of carts slipped down the mountain!

We would tumble down onto each other, hitting the frozen ground; the carts tipped over, the stones spilled out, and it almost always happened that at least one of us broke a hand, a nose, or a foot.

To top off this whole ordeal, we also had to witness the terrible scenes in the pit. People who had been caught in houses were taken there and shot. After the murder, the Germans used a "tractor" of sorts, with the shovel carrying the dead person and tossing him into a pit near the mountain on which we were working. Then they burned the bodies; the cold night air carried the odor of the charred flesh and bone from the pit and filled the air around us with a nauseating stench that made it all the more difficult for us.

There were those who tried to escape. In such cases, the entire camp suffered. A *selektion* was announced, and everyone had to rush to the *appelplatz*, where each person had to carry a very heavy plank and stand in front of the monster who gazed into the face of each and every one of us. Anyone who didn't seem stable and strong enough while holding the plank was shot on the spot.

He made sure to spill Jewish blood every single day. We were deathly afraid every time he entered the camp. We knew he was going to shoot someone! We would also absorb beatings during food distribution. So in addition to the backbreaking labor, we were constantly experiencing punishments and brutal *selektions*.

Despite all the suffering, three of us women from Tarnow

supported each other. We all tried to keep kosher. If they put a donkey bone into the pot—we didn't eat that day. We were still infused with strength from our glorious pasts; the warm flame of our parents' homes had not been extinguished.

14

FROM THE DEPTHS OF DESPAIR

Five weeks before Purim 5704/1944.

Dawn broke, and we hobbled back from our nighttime work shift.

Suddenly, we were surrounded by Germans. "Follow us!" they barked, and hustled us into a side room. We didn't understand why. What had we done? What were they planning for us now?

We just wanted to get back to our barracks, but we weren't given permission. Finally they offered some information: "You're being transferred."

Some time before, a group from our camp in Plashow was sent to the Skarzysko camp in Poland. The main thing was not to let us stay in one place for too long! That was one of the Germans' methods. Now, we were going to be sent away.

Ahead of our transfer, I was once again assailed by loneliness. I was so alone! Without a brother, sister, or even a dear friend.

Just a few women who I knew from the Tarnow ghetto, but they weren't Orthodox.

Ida was one of them. She had been brought to Poland from Germany during the deportation of 1938. I knew her from the Tarnow ghetto, and here in the camp she was very devoted to me.

We spent a whole night in that isolated room, and the loneliness and uncertainty were acute. At one point, several prisoners broke the wall that divided our room from the next one—and we discovered huge piles of clothes. All those who had come to Plashow had been ordered to undress—and here were the clothes.

"L'olam tikach—always take," we thought to ourselves, and began to do just that. We had bread sacks that we took to work with us each night. Now we filled these sacks with various garments. We didn't know if we'd be allowed to keep them, but for now, we took them. People wrapped themselves in several layers of clothing. I also took a black velvet garment and put it into my bag.

The next day they led us out of the room to the train station. We were pushed into train cars, not knowing where we were being taken. It's not like we could ask, or express an opinion! They did with us whatever they wanted, unimpeded.

We were taken to Chenstochow—a labor camp comprised of stone structures, not barracks. We were interned there, but there was no work for us. After a week, we were ordered back onto the trains. We were on the move again.

A Whole Loaf of Bread

We were given a whole loaf of bread as food for the journey. How long had it been since we had seen a whole loaf of bread?! Eons…

Hunger ravaged the prisoners. It was impossible to describe the hunger! I remember the prisoners who had declared while still in Plashow: "We don't want to die of hunger. We want to sit near a table with a whole loaf of bread and a knife, so we can slice off as much bread as we want. Just not to die of hunger!"

And now, in Chenstochow, we were given an entire loaf of bread and a pat of margarine.

There were two types of prisoners among us. There were those who said, "We'll eat the bread now and feel full!" They did not think of the future and chose to enjoy the present.

Others decided to divide the bread so they could save some for the coming days.

I belonged to the latter group. "I won't eat a whole loaf of bread at once!" I decided. "It's enough for a whole month, and I can subsist on this bread for that long!"

And I kept my treasure in my sack, guarding it carefully.

The trip was dreadful. We were transported in cattle cars. Finally we reached the Skarzysko camp, just a few kilometers from Warsaw.

The camp had been in operation for two or three years already. People had been brought there from the Warsaw ghetto a long time before. There were "veteran" inmates who had already experienced Majdanek. Others came from Shedlitz and Lodz.

For us, it was another step deeper into Gehinnom…

Our welcome was brutal, including slaps on the face, curses and vulgarities by the camp directors, Jewish and non-Jewish alike.

Snow began to fall and accumulate on the ground. It was a week before Purim and Poland was still in a deep freeze.

We weren't taken to a barrack. We stood for a whole day on the wet snow, our mood matching the weather perfectly.

And here, too, there was a ray of light!

The bread…the bread we had received in Chenstochow…at least we had what to eat.

Night had already fallen when the Lagerführer arrived and began to howl: "Lazy women! Why are you standing here outside?"

"Where should we stand? Where should we go?" we replied. "We are new here. We were brought here and no one lets us in."

"I'll show you, you lazy good-for-nothings!" he screeched. "You'll see there's room!"

He began to kick and drag us. Each one was asked separately: "Where do you want to go?"

There were three barracks, A, B, and C.

Without much thought, I said I wanted to go to A.

I was frozen and exhausted. I wanted to just get inside, to the closest place. So A was as good a place as any...

We were taken to the barracks, and had to stand like paupers at the door and beg to be let in. While standing there, I discovered five women that I knew from Tarnow!

"Quick!" the Lagerführer shouted to the *blockelteste*. "Make room for these five women!"

"Where?" she replied. "All the places are taken! There is no room!"

Instead of an answer, the monster delivered two ringing slaps with his truncheon to the most senior official in the barrack, the *blockelteste*, in front of everyone. "Make them room right away!" he thundered.

Without a word, she climbed up to the top bunks, ordered several women to get down, and said, "Now there's room."

We were sent up to the top tier of bunks.

The atmosphere in the camp was hellish.

We got there after a typhus epidemic that had devoured the camp population. It had broken out due to the terrible hunger, and people fell like flies. Despair gnawed at everyone.

The prisoners wore clothes made of paper, because there was nothing else.

Dead bodies were strewn everywhere, and people stepped on them. No one even hesitated, or recoiled, from examining the bodies to see if there were perhaps gold crowns on the teeth. In exchange for a piece of gold, they could receive a slice of bread from the Polish laborers.

Among the dead, there were those who had hidden diamonds on their person when they had come into the camps. They had sewn them into various places, and after they died in the epidemic, the survivors searched the bodies in an effort to find something of value that could be of use to them.

The chilling scenes were too hard for us to witness.

The Rat's Visit

The night was snowy. I lay, exhausted, in the barrack, after standing for so long in the snow. Finally, I was offered someplace to sleep. I lay and thought about my bread. Where could I hide it so it should not get lost or stolen? Finally, I put it into the sack, which I placed beneath my head, and it also served as a pillow.

Lying there that night on the top bunk late that snowy night, I comforted myself with thoughts of my bread. Just thinking about how much bread I had made me feel more satiated.

That night, an unexpected guest paid a visit.

It was a huge hungry rat. Even the rodents didn't have what to eat in the camp. It came to our barrack and began to wreak havoc. Among other things, it tore off a piece of my bread.

I didn't dare complain, because it had taken only my bread. One of the girls got her toe bitten off—that's how hungry the rat was.

I gazed at my bread with revulsion. A rat had touched it! I

pushed it away, nauseated by the thought. At the time, I was still so particular about this kind of thing; in time, that passed as well.

The girl who had lost her toe wailed in pain and anguish over what the rat had done to her.

The next "welcome" that I had was having my towel and a pair of socks stolen. When I went to work, I left them on my plank, and when I returned I saw that it had all been stolen. From then on, I took everything I had wherever I went—if I had anything at that time.

There was a woman in our barrack who had come from Warsaw. Until the war, she belonged to the aristocratic elite there—her sister was one of the main actresses in the Warsaw theater.

But here, the woman sank to such tremendous depths despite her status! She was afflicted with lice that penetrated her skin and tortured her.

No one showered at Skarzysko; there wasn't enough water. In Plashow there were taps in the bathrooms and we could shower. Here, the only option—for those with *protektsia*—was to go to the kitchen to get a bit of water.

Among those in the camp were prisoners who had already experienced two years of torture here, and before that, had suffered through the Warsaw Ghetto and Majdanek.

In Majdanek, they told anyone who wanted to work to report to the assembly area. People had nothing to lose, and those who volunteered were brought here, to Skarzysko.

They envied us for having just arrived...

They were mired in despair. In their presence, we were not allowed to express a shred of hope that perhaps we might survive. They simply forbid anyone to hope for anything!

Compassion Amid Judgment

One night, I sat on my bunk and thought about the approaching Pesach. The year before, I was still with my mother, sisters, and little brother, and we had held a clandestine Seder.

What would be here? Pesach would begin in two days. I could not bear the thought that there would be no holiday, no Seder, nothing…

I was sure that somewhere in the camp, matzos were being baked; I surmised that I could probably even obtain a piece. I resolved to ask the veteran inmates. They could tell me what had happened last year.

I turned to one of them with a question: "It's Erev Pesach. Does anyone bake matzos here?"

She looked at me with endless pain in her eyes and then began to scream: "What are you thinking? In such circumstances, you are dreaming about baking matzos? They should be hanged, those girls who came from Tarnow…" she added.

Indeed, we were still relatively reasonable compared to them. One of us, for example, was still fussy enough and hadn't tasted a morsel of food aside from the bread she had brought with her.

The poor veterans here could not bear our "normalcy." They found it hard to see that someone was still thinking positively, hoping and believing, even in this desperate situation.

"You still believe in those ancient things? Come, let's kill you, we'll shoot you," they hissed.

After the war, I learned that there actually was a Rebbe in the Skarzysko camp, and that indeed, matzos had been baked in one of the corners of the ghetto!

I didn't think of going to look. Every night, we returned from work so drained and exhausted—not to mention starving—that we couldn't even think of where to start looking for matzos. After all, I had merely asked and the answer I received was so terrible.

Standing on my swollen legs, I felt that I just couldn't do it anymore!

The work I was doing was extremely difficult. My job now was to prepare a certain number of bullets that were to be stored in weapons. I wasn't familiar with the machine, which was very old fashioned. It kept getting stuck and stopped working. I didn't know how to open it to unjam it.

A supervisor walked among the workers to make sure that the work was being carried out properly and that the output was meeting quotas, but I was totally unsuited for this kind of work. Standing for twelve hours straight was unbearable, and there was no option to sit. My legs were swollen as the result of my prior difficult work in the stone quarry, where I also developed terrible rheumatism. It was actually the brutal combination of the extended standing and the rheumatism that caused the painful swelling.

I couldn't bend my knees under any circumstances. When we walked to work, we marched four or five women abreast, and my friends, who knew me from Tarnow, walked on either side of me and helped support me. They held me under my arms and literally dragged me, because I couldn't walk.

Ida, my dear friend, worked especially hard to support me, but did not survive the war. She could not eat the dirty food we were given and died of hunger. May Hashem remember her for good.

A Day Off

There was a small medical clinic in the camp. Rumor had it that for a payment we could obtain a note from the doctor that we had high fever of over 38 degrees Celsius, and we could stay in the barrack for a day and not go to work.

I dreamed of resting for a day from work, and I was able to, *baruch Hashem*. I still had the black velvet garment I had brought with me from Plashow; I sold it to a non-Jew and earned a bit of money. At Skarzysko, we could trade a bit on the illegal black market. Thus I was able to obtain enough money to bribe the doctor.

I went to the clinic and told the doctor I suffered from terrible rheumatism. Fortunately, my temperature was indeed above 38 degrees, and the note I received from the doctor allowed me to remain "home" for one day. He added, "If you had money, I could also prescribe shots that would ease your discomfort a bit."

I didn't have any money so that possibility was out of the question. But at least I had that day of rest from work. Each day, the Jewish supervisors would patrol the barracks to see if anyone had stayed in bed. They found me lying down and came over with their sticks raised, ready to beat me.

I took out my note and showed it to them. The supervisor backed off and went on his way.

I rested for that one single day, but it gave me a bit of strength.

The tears poured from my eyes like a river. There were no chairs in the camp, and I had to stand for twelve hours straight each day, suffering in pain. I had to bend over holding a heavy shovel and shovel into a receiving compartment, and make sure that the machine was working properly. I just couldn't do it!

Divine *Hashgachah* sent me an angel from Above: Fela, a young girl from Krakow who had come to the camp from an orphanage.

She worked beside me and saw the tears streaming from my eyes. "What's wrong with you?" she asked compassionately.

I shared my secret with her: "I can barely stand on my swollen legs! I can't bend my knees and I have no strength to deal with this machine."

The first thing she did was switch places with me. Until then, I was first in line and Fela was second. When there was an inspection, the supervisor usually checked the first machine in the line, and she used a certain device to detect if the requisite number of bullets had been produced. In order for the bullet fire to be effective, the bullet had to fit exactly. If it was too wide or narrow, the bullet would not travel in a straight trajectory and would miss the target...

Beyond that, a very cruel overseer walked among the girls and beat them left and right for no reason, claiming they were not producing enough and that the bullets were not of good quality.

Dear Fela did a tremendous *chesed* by changing places with me. In addition, she told me, "You don't do anything. Just stand and pretend you are working." She did my work in addition to her own! She filled the machine with material for me, and prepared the daily quota.

After some years, when I told my husband, the Rebbe, about this wonderful girl, he was surprised at me. "Why didn't you find out the girl's full name, so that you could pay her back after the war?"

Hashem should reward the young, angelic girl who took so much pity on me.

It was another ray of light in the darkness, during a period when humanity declined to a nadir and people thought only of themselves. In such a horrific situation, I encountered the purity of the Jewish soul. I witnessed the *tzelem Elokim*, the compassion that still flickered beneath all the troubles and torture.

Fela, the orphan girl, did not know me from before. She had led a difficult life even before arriving in the camp—and look how much compassion she displayed, and how she had saved me! May Hashem repay her for her good!

A Flourishing, Sad Spring

The condition of us residents of Barrack A was relatively good. The prisoners in Barrack C worked with radiation-emitting chemical materials. They became frighteningly thin and yellow; their hair turned red from the radiation exposure, and their overall appearance was appalling. The materials that were used to fill underground mines was called picrin. They were poisoned by the picrin and died within a very short time.

Every so often we had to give in our clothes to be disinfected. Perhaps that was a blessing in disguise, because otherwise, the lice would have eaten us alive.

Slowly, the Polish spring began to emerge. Each day, we walked to work—G-d forbid we should ride in a vehicle—surrounded by pretty scenery. We passed Polish villages where we saw flowers blooming in magical colors. The trees budded and bloomed, and the spring flowering was at its peak.

Tears would flood my eyes. *The world is so beautiful,* I would think. *Spring is here and we are in such depths of despair! In this Gehinnom, in the valley of death—among the delicious smelling flowers and budding trees. The machines are rumbling all around us, and the evil Nazis, who ooze with cruelty, surround us. There is constant danger hanging over our heads...*

Even when we returned "home" to the barracks, the atmosphere was very difficult. The value of life had plummeted. People died like flies and their bodies were assaulted by those searching for gold teeth and other valuables. And of course it was forbidden to display a ray of hope...

B'chasdei Hashem, I had my friend Ida and a few other girls from Tarnow, and I was able to survive the loneliness. The other prisoners persecuted us and envied us to no end. "You were still with your parents last year," they would say constantly. "We've been in this hell on earth for two years already."

I spent just a few months in Skarzysko. In a sense, it was easier than in the earlier camp—anyone who had money could purchase things through the gentile workers—but the unbearable atmosphere weighed me down terribly, and was compounded by the raging typhus epidemic there.

In time, I reached the conclusion that had I been at Skarzysko one month more, I could not have survived it any longer.

Summer 5704/1944 approached and the Germans began absorbing loss after loss on the Russian front. One day, we learned that the Russians were drawing near, and even Lublin had been restored to Polish hands.

The commanders of the Skarzysko camp did not know what to do with us. For two or three days they didn't send us to work. The days were warm, and there was a lot of sand all around us.

Suddenly I had an idea: the sand was warmed by the sun, and I could take advantage of this to ease my rheumatism!

I dug space for my two swollen legs in the sand, which was very beneficial. The swelling went down and I felt much better.

> *I went out into the pleasant sun, and walked home slowly to summon Chaya to school.*

An alleyway in Tarnow.

> *"Operate?! Chalilah! Travel to Krakow right away!" the Rebbe ordered decisively.*

The Rebbe, Rav Yitzchak Horowitz, *zt"l*, of Stutchin

The city was burning, the skies stained a horrific orange color. The Bais Medrash, which had been standing for some four hundred years, went up in flames.

The Central *Bais Medrash* in Tarnow.

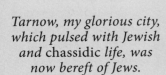

Tarnow, my glorious city, which pulsed with Jewish and chassidic life, was now bereft of Jews.

The bimah that remained in the shul, a silent remnant of a glorious past.

"Ribbono shel Olam,"
I uttered silently,
"Have the fates of my
mother and sisters also
been sealed? Is there
something I should
be doing? What is
required of me now?"

The deportation of the Jews of Tarnow.

Wise Rivka'le managed
to smuggle her way
back into the ghetto the
same way she got out.

The entrance to the Tarnow ghetto.

I knew every corner
in Tarnow, every
curve of the road. I
ran as fast as I could,
but that madman
caught up to me, and
the "incriminating"
book was still in my
hands.

A street in Tarnow.

The window of his room would suddenly open, and his evil eyes would follow us, the stone workers, as we performed slave labor.

The porch from where the wicked Amon Goethe, *ym"s*, watched the workers of the quarry in the Plashow camp.

Songs of hope, stones rolling down the slope, frozen nights and eyes desperate for sleep… These are the flashes of memory that I have from the stone quarry in Plashow.

The Plashow concentration camp in those days.

This incident left its impression forever, my "souvenir" from Plashow that would scar my hand from then on, and a small, permanent burn on my face.

The Plashow concentration camp today.

119

15

WANTED: THE COLOR RED

"For your own good," the "benevolent" Germans told us, "From today, you will not be going to work. We will take you to Germany and there you will work in factories similar to those here in Skarzysko, and with the same type of machines. It is wartime now, and your work is valuable to us."

As usual, they were misleading us.

They began the transfer with a horrific *selektion*. Everyone was ordered to gather in a specific location, and the Lagerführer stood in front of us holding a long stick, with a huge dog at his side. The dog was almost as big as he was. Each one of us had to pass before him.

The older women were especially afraid. There was a twenty-year-old girl from Tarnow among us, and she was very pale. The girls looked all over to find a piece of paper with red ink in order to rub some color into her skin.

We all headed for the gathering place, trembling in fear. The beast gazed into our faces and decided if the prisoner was healthy enough to remain alive or not. It was enough to hear that murderer, to look at his dogs—the one on two legs and the one on four—to make one go pale as plaster.

The red coloring did not help. Even beyond the artificial coloring, the paleness of our faces was apparent. Tragically, that young girl from Tarnow was dragged out of the line and shot on the spot.

In addition, some of the people taken out of the line were pushed into a vehicle standing nearby, where they were poisoned with gas and burned to death. A prisoner who registered as being sick for two weeks was automatically placed in that vehicle. People were very careful to hide the fact that they were sick.

At the end of the *selektion*, all those who were left were pushed into cattle cars, at least one hundred people to a car. They crushed more and more people in, until we were literally like sardines in a can. There was hardly room to stand. We had no food or drink, nor the basic human amenities. The windows were barred with barbed wire.

The journey lasted four days. Most of the time, the train stood in one place because the tracks had been bombed out in many places. It was dark and stuffy inside the cars, we were starving and thirsty, and we weren't given food or drink.

At the train stations, Polish passengers strolled along placidly. "Give us a bit of water!" we pleaded. Occasionally, someone had pity on us and brought a large vessel of water. He would push the water to us from between the stairs, in a small cup, in exchange for a few zloty or something else of value. If the Germans noticed this, they ran quickly over to the train and spilled all the water onto the ground. The trip seemed to last an eternity, but finally, the train reached its destination.

It was a week before Rosh Hashanah 5705. We didn't know where we were being taken, but based on the signposting in German, we surmised that we had arrived in Germany.

We quickly discovered that we had been taken to an extermination camp near Leipzig. For us, a new depth in this Gehinnom on earth opened.

When we disembarked from the train, we noticed Polish women wearing a certain type of clothing. The prisoners among us, who had already "graduated" from Majdenek, pulled at their hair: "Gevald! There's a crematorium here, too!" they wailed. They were familiar with the type of workers needed in such a camp and trembled in fear. They realized that this was no labor camp, but rather, a death camp.

We were ordered into the showers. The girls were terrified; in Majdanek people had also been told they were taking showers, and were then sprayed with gas that killed them…

They didn't want to believe that these were water showers. "There they also told us to shower; it's a trick. We know what these showers are about, and what a crematorium is," they sobbed.

My friend Poriya, a native of Warsaw, told me what they had experienced in Majdanek and why they were so frightened. "I came from the Warsaw ghetto to Majdanek with my mother and sister. Every day, prisoners were taken to the crematorium and burned. One day they announced that anyone who wanted, could volunteer for work. We had nothing to lose so some of us signed up. That's how I got to the labor camp with you, and I was spared. And now, again…"

We all believed that these were our final moments and decided to eat whatever remaining food we had.

Why Should the Gentiles Be Able to Say...

The doctor arrived; she was as frightening as the devil, and she held a shaving machine in her hand. Anyone who was found to have even one louse in her head was shaved right away.

My friends and I hoped not to be shaved! Please, not that... We didn't want them to say that the Jewish women were lowly, dirty, and lice infested. There were many gentiles in the camps from different countries such as France, Belgium, and Yugoslavia. There were some who had been arrested as partisans in the Ukraine, Poland, Bulgaria, and Hungary among others. We didn't want to feel inferior among them...

After the shower (which was, indeed, just a shower), each one of us was inspected by flashlight. I was trembling like a leaf, because I was covered in terribly infected sores, especially beneath my armpits from when my friends held me there to help me walk. But a miracle happened! It was as though the doctor was blinded. With great *siyata diShmaya*, she did not discover my sores. She checked every hair, but did not find any lice and left my hair intact.

The Germans confiscated everything we had. They searched for gold and other valuables that people may have hidden in their clothes.

We stood for an entire day, hearing repeated announcements: "Anyone who left a gold watch, a gold ring, diamonds, or any other valuables in their clothes should come and tell us." But it was to no avail. No one came forth. I still hear the echoes of those repeated calls.

There were married women among us. One of them gave birth in the camp just before the liberation. After the war, I met her in Switzerland with her daughter, as I will relate later on.

At this point, we were allowed into the huts, but we didn't

get any clothes. After a few days we received garments stamped with numbers. Now we were converted into numbers, nameless and with no identity. Fortunately, numbers were not etched into our skin, like they were in Auschwitz and in other camps.

We were overseen by German-speaking Polish women. Despite the fact that some of them were intelligent and knowledgeable, their education did not change their essence. They were cruel and tortured us constantly. When they distributed the bread, they stole slices for themselves; they gave us smaller portions and treated us with extreme brutality.

Each day, attendance was taken under the open sky, as we all stood. They counted us, and if the Germans imagined that the number was not right—they counted us again and again, and we had to stand on our aching legs until the numbers were right to them.

My Precious Pictures!

They took away my clothes, but left my socks and shoes on my feet. I was happy that my pictures were with me and found comfort in them. The pictures accompanied me throughout my ordeal, beginning in 1942.

In the summer of 5702, while we were still in the Tarnow ghetto, my father surprised us. "By *erliche Yidden*, it is not accepted to take photographs. But now, we don't know where we will be sent and where we will end up, we should at least have a memory of the family. I want us all to take pictures."

My father invited a photographer and we posed for a photo. Everyone received one copy of the photo. The picture was invaluable to me, and it was the only personal possession I retained throughout my travels and ordeals.

I had another photo of the children of the Tarnow ghetto, *Hy"d*, who had attended our secret kindergarten.

I hid these two treasures in my socks.

One night, after we lay down to sleep, I hid my two pairs of socks, with the pictures, in a sack. In the morning, I left my items on my bunk, and when I returned, the socks with the photos were gone.

My precious photos! How anguished I was by their loss!

I suspect that the Polish *blockelteste* had stolen them. In the mornings, when the barracks were empty and we were at work, she would rummage around in our sacks, seeking valuables. She didn't need my pictures, only diamonds, gold and silver, but still, she stole my precious treasure. In addition to the torture administered by the Germans, we suffered from the other gentiles around us as well.

The Polish and Ukrainian prisoners suffered like we did, but they had pride. They felt satisfaction at being imprisoned because they had fought for their homelands. For three days and nights, those prisoners refused to go to work in protest. They were finally successful and sent for light work in the kitchen or laundry, not in the factories, and in the interim, they enjoyed harassing us.

It was terrible, dreadful—but I had Poriya and Gita, my dear friends from Bais Yaakov. Being with them saved me from the depths of despair in Leipzig.

In the earlier camps I had devoted friends, but they were not *frum* like me. Poriya and Gita felt like sisters.

On Rosh Hashanah 5705, we were told that there would be a lice check again. This time, it was only for the Jewish prisoners. If a louse would be found, we were told, our heads would be shaved.

We felt a sense of mission coursing through us: to save our Jewish dignity! We were determined that they not find lice and not shave us! We could not allow the gentile women to stare scornfully at our shaved heads.

We checked each other's heads, picking out the lice, and hoping with all our might that they wouldn't gloat that the Jewesses were lice infested.

Baruch Hashem, my friends and I went through the war with our hair on our heads. That was also a ray of light, because in Auschwitz, for example, every single prisoner was shorn.

In the Metal Factory

One day the block supervisor was instructed to prepare a group of the strongest, healthiest women to be sent for very difficult work in the factory.

She didn't bother to check how strong and able we were to do hard work. She just walked over to a corner and gathered as many women as she needed and wrote down their numbers.

My friends—Poriya (Sokol, author of *Black Tracks in the Snow*), and Gita (Tova Silberberg), myself, and other friends, all of us delicate, weak girls, were part of her quota.

Our new work was called "*di golvenishe upteiling*." It was Sisyphean work, under terrible conditions of starvation.

"You should know," the Germans had warned the Polish youths who had worked there before us, "people belonging to the most inferior nation are going to arrive here, and you are not allowed to make any contact with them!"

I don't want to mention the explicit term the Germans used to describe us.

One Polish boy violated the order, and dared to tell us: "Don't live with the illusion that you will be able to stand it here. I came here as part of a group of 500 men, and almost all of them have died. Me and two or three others are still alive. The work is too hard to be able to do it and survive."

The Polish workers were lucky enough to live in houses and

they had as much food as they wanted, which they received in an organized fashion. We, on the other hand, received only the slice of bread and soup, and at night we got a cup of coffee—which was one step up from the previous camp.

Once a month, we received a dairy soup—which was considered a big treat.

The *meister*, the supervisor, who oversaw the work was a very old man. He wasn't the worst of them, but he always told us, "I am living through hell in this world because I have to work with Jews." Still, he didn't beat us too much for no reason.

He treated the gentile workers kindly. Once, a ring belonging to one of them fell into a deep pool. He ordered the pool emptied so she could get her ring back. There was no chance that any such benevolence would be displayed toward the Jewish prisoners.

Working alongside the *meister* was a female SS supervisor who was extremely cruel. She would beat us for no reason, and would walk among us and lash out randomly with her truncheon. The sadism shone on her face, and she enjoyed administering the beatings as the *meister* stood passively on the side.

We worked right next to a huge pool. In the middle of the factory were barbed wires that went round and round, like a carousel. We had to dip bombs into caustic chemical baths to protect them from heat and fire. The bombs were very heavy and probably meant to be launched from planes. They were hunks of metal, shaped like pipes, with two wheels on the underside. We dipped them into very deep pools. Pool after pool. Dip after dip. It was a huge exertion, in our weakened state, to lift these heavy metal things and dip them into various dangerous substances, either boiling or freezing.

I cannot fathom how I was able to withstand the weight, taking into consideration the terrible conditions in which we lived.

A Bit Longer, It Will Come

On the first day at our new job dipping the bombs into the chemicals, I was severely burned. On the second day, we were given long gloves, one set made of cotton and one of rubber, but for me, it was too late.

I lifted the heavy metal pole with the little bit of energy that I had, in order to dip it into the mixture. Unfortunately, I had not dipped it deeply enough into the chlorinated water, and it bounced back at me, spraying me with the chemical, which splattered onto my face, hands and clothes and leaving its mark on me forever. I remained with a permanent mark on my hand and a small scar on my face.

The burns felt like live fire. Yet, with all the pain, I recognized the miracle I had experienced: Had the substance gone anywhere near my eyes, I would have been blinded.

But to my horror, the garment I was wearing began to disintegrate from the harsh chemical. My body burned like it was aflame, and if you think I was given a new garment to replace it, you are mistaken.

For many weeks, an argument raged between the soldiers overseeing the factory and the camp directors. Each one claimed that the other side had to give me a new garment. The Germans hadn't anticipated the number of Jews they would be able to stuff into the camps, and they didn't think they'd need so many uniforms, and thus there was a shortage then.

On the front, the Germans were sustaining loss after loss and were retreating from the Russians. The latter were capturing extensive swathes of territory, and half of Poland was in Russian hands. They had already reached Auschwitz and were heading west. We didn't know about the Germans' extensive losses and that there was a shortage of uniforms. When they built the camps, they didn't plan on such resounding success in concentrating so many Jews into them.[1]

The argument continued for a few weeks until they deigned to give me an overall made of prickly material. Today, they use this fabric for certain kinds of "itchy" blankets made for the winter.

The material really bothered me. I had always had sensitive skin, and even more so in the summer. I couldn't deal with the heat and the itchiness. I suffered terribly from the baking summer sun.

"Soon autumn will come," my friends soothed me over and over. "Soon autumn will come, and then winter, and you'll have a warm garment. You'll be warm and you'll be happy with it."

And truthfully, autumn and its chill did arrive, and what did that bring?

When the weather began to change—the fiends took the garment away from me, and replaced it with something thin and flimsy. They were constantly finding ways to make us as miserable as possible.

Now I was as cold as everyone else, but my friends' comforting words continued to warm me...

Not a Single Potato

The Ukrainians, who were the worst anti-Semites, tortured us especially. The Germans gave them instructions and utilized the Ukrainians to harass the Jews.

According to "racial theory," Poles were one level above Jews; Russians were one level above that, and the Ukrainians, a few levels above. That's why they were deemed "worthy" of torturing us. The Ukrainians were obsessed with making trouble for us. For example, at first, the workers were not divided by groups and

---

1. The Sassover Rebbe of Monsey, *shlita*, a son, notes: My mother even judged the Germans favorably. In time it became known that the Germans had an abundance of clothes they had confiscated from the Jews of Hungary.

we all stood in one long line—Jews and Poles—to get our daily portion of soup. The lucky ones among us got a potato or two in the soup, while the rest sufficed with cloudy water.

One day, the Ukrainians who worked in the kitchen announced: "Things will not continue this way. Poles and Jews must be separated." Although they were prisoners like us, they separated us and divided the food according to blocks in which the prisoners slept. Their order was non-negotiable: Poles came first and Jews would come afterwards; this way they guaranteed that no Jews got any potatoes.

Standing at the head of the Jewish line I could hear them calling, "Oh, *di Yiddishe kinder gein yetzt*—the Jews are coming." If it seemed that an errant potato would get into our soup, they immediately returned it to the pot and switched pots to one that certainly had only water.

The Poles were also wicked. By contrast, the Yugoslavian workers treated us much better. They were partisans who fought the Germans, and didn't harass us.

Beside me worked a Czech gentile woman; she wasn't too bad. She and her husband were Communists. When I fasted on Yom Kippur she made sure I didn't work too hard. She was old enough to be my mother, and perhaps indeed, she felt a need to watch over me.

These rays of humanity shone through everything, and it is important to record them for posterity.

16

THE TORCH OF BAIS YAAKOV
LIGHTS UP THE DARKNESS

The prisoners worked around me in silence. They had been sent to the labor camp in Leipzig from all over Europe after years of suffering in ghettos and other camps. It wasn't the first stop on my own travails during the Holocaust, but here, it was so different: I had my dear friends by my side. A wonderful ray of light shone through the horrible labor camp. The dear Bais Yaakov girls were company for me. We hadn't known each other before the war, but now, we united under one invisible banner: "Bnos Bais Yaakov." We were a group of girls—friends and acquaintances—as well as a former Bais Yaakov teacher from Tarnow. We also had a Rebbetzin, the daughter of the Modzhitzer Rebbe.

It was my personal *gan eden* in the German Gehinnom.

One of my biggest challenges on my earlier stops during the

war years was overcoming the difficulties when I was surrounded by people who were hostile to religion. There were places where I didn't have a single *frum* friend.

That wasn't the case in the camp in Leipzig: Bais Yaakov seemed to have been transplanted from the placid villages to the gates of Gehinnom. Despite the difficult work I was assigned, dipping the metals into dangerous chemicals, I was warmed by the light of the torch of Bais Yaakov, and we were able to overcome the difficulties with faith and hope.

Looking back, it's hard to believe it, but even during those darkest days, when we were shattered and exhausted from the backbreaking work and all the dreadful experiences, we would have a little "*shiur*" of sorts. In addition, after work, all us *heimish* girls would sit together and try to provide support and encouragement to one another.

Birkas Hachodesh

"Tomorrow, we bentsch the *chodesh!* Do you hear, girls? Rosh Chodesh *bentschen!*"

The news spread, seemingly dancing from one girl to the next. Just like we chewed our bread over and over, making sure to grind each crumb thoroughly before it made its way down our throats, so too, the news played on our starving ears, tinkling with an otherworldly song; it had been so long since we'd heard those notes. Then they made their way from our ears to our souls—our tortured souls that so longed for something in the depths that we found ourselves.

It had been years since our souls had been satiated by organized *tefillah.* They hadn't said "*Elokai neshamah shenasata bi,*" because under the German boot, in the panic of the work and the gnawing hunger, who even remembered?

That Friday, like the days that had preceded it, we had no idea where we were standing in the world. What was the date, what month was it? Suddenly we noticed new prisoners who had arrived in a transport from Hungary who were still sane, and they remembered. They had been expelled from their homes years after we were. They still kept track of the Jewish calendar.

One of them hissed towards two Jewish girls:

"Tomorrow we *bentsch* the month of Shevat. Rosh Chodesh is on Wednesday."

The girls almost froze in place. No, they were not allowed to stand still—they had to keep walking so as not to cast suspicion on anyone. But that Hungarian Jew had said something electrifying, and the message had to be conveyed immediately to the Rebbetzin, the Modzhitzer Rebbe's daughter, who was with us in the camp!

And that's how we got the wonderful news.

"Girls, we'll have to find a way to gather in the cellar and *bentsch* the *chodesh*. Before work or afterwards, *b'ezras Hashem*, we will *bentsch* the *chodesh*."

I don't recall exactly how we were able to do it. Perhaps they didn't send us to work that day. There were days when the Germans wanted to spare themselves the food distribution and made us stay in our barracks.

We gathered. The Rebbetzin said the *tefillah* by heart, and we repeated it after her.

It was the only time we *bentsched* the *chodesh* in the camp in Leipzig.

We were so cut off from normal life that I didn't even say *Modeh Ani* in the camps. Maybe it was because I didn't wash my hands. I didn't even remember *Kriyas Shema*! My friend Poriyah told me that she had written the words of *Kriyas Shema* down for herself and that's how she remembered. We weren't allowed to carry pen or paper, and we were closely watched to make sure that we had nothing in our possession; nevertheless, Poriyah succeeded in writing the *parshiyos* down on a scrap of paper and hid the note in her straw mattress. "I was afraid that one day, I would forget *Kriyas Shema*," she confided, "and that's why I did it."

The *Shakla Vetarya* on the Bonuses

"Is it permitted or not? What do you say, Poriyah?"

"It's *pikuach nefesh*."

"Why is that? We managed the whole month without dairy soup. We'll manage today, too."

"But they only give it out once a month. Will we be alive by the next distribution?"

"There is an issue of *mekach* and *memchar*, dealing, with bonuses and that's a problem on Shabbos."

"It's not really a purchase."

"I'm hungry."

"You can overcome it."

It was a serious, in-depth discussion. The labor camp closed its residents in with barbed wire, and in one of the blocks a group of girls sat debating a matter of *hilchos Shabbos*. It was a real "*shakla vetarya*," back and forth debate.

It all started the day our commander decided that we were doing truly dreadful work, and therefore, we deserved "valuable papers" that he called "bonuses."

"After the war, these papers will be worth a lot of money," he told us. "You'll be able to get money at German banks for them." Those, of course, were tall tales. But in the camp itself, we could buy ourselves something with those papers from time to time, whether it was a toothbrush or wooden clogs. I had very worn out shoes, so I bought myself a pair of Dutch shoes, with big heels.

These shoes saved me in the future (see Chapter 19).

One Friday night, upon our return from work, we were informed that we could get dairy soup in exchange for our bonuses.

This was a bombshell for us: the dairy soup was considered extremely valuable, but we were not allowed to buy anything on Shabbos!

I remember the debate as though it took place yesterday. We sat around with Shifra Singer (Yudasin); Poriyah, whose faith was rock-solid; and the Nirbator Rebbetzin. We thought and discussed, deliberating back and forth until we decided: "No! We would not buy the dairy soup on Shabbos. We would control ourselves and not stumble on what might possibly be an *issur*..."

The camp provided us with countless opportunities to overcome challenges. When they distributed a bit of dairy coffee to us right after we ate soup that had been cooked with meat— we didn't drink the coffee right away. We decided to wait. I don't know if we waited six hours between meat and milk; but we tried to wait, and made the effort to separate meat from milk.

An Expression of Human Emotion

It was New Year's Eve, December 31, 1944.

The Nazi sentries had abandoned their lookout posts, and even the Polish supervisors had gone to celebrate the new year. Before they left, they told us in Yiddish, "*Kinder*, this is the only time we let you do whatever you want!"

We already knew beforehand that we would have a free night to ourselves. We decided to devote the time to a "social evening." We gathered all the *frum* girls and a group of girls from Jewish homes who were affiliated with the Haskalah movement. Prominent among them were the Carmel sisters, who were known to be very talented. The two, who came from a *frum* home, would compose moving songs about life in the camps and about the past that was no longer.

We sat and listened to the songs they had composed for the evening. Ayala Carmel was known as the "singer of the camp." She composed many songs, which were both moving and maudlin. Among other melodies, she sang a wonderful song in which she mourned her father: "*Un dem Tatten's seforim shtub.*" She lamented her father's treasured *seforim* that had been lost, and described how the tongues of flame had licked at the bookshelves and turned the treasure into a pile of ash.

With talent and deep emotion, she cried to us that she would never find herself bent over the headstone of her father. She did not know what day he was taken to his bitter fate, nor the location of his resting place. Her words powerfully expressed the image of Germany as one massive camp surrounded by gates of barbed wire.

In another song, she expressed her pain by saying, "We didn't want to go to Eretz Yisrael, we were afraid to work hard; now we are exhausted and doing backbreaking work, but not for our Holy Land."

The Carmel sisters survived the war with their mother. Tragically, during the liberation in Germany, an Allied tank unintentionally rolled over one of their legs, and it had to be amputated. She received excellent care by the Allied forces, but remained crippled for life. Later, the two emigrated to the United States with their mother. I heard that they received a certificate of excellence for a book they wrote in English about the Holocaust.

That free evening we had was wonderful, and we were able to express the human emotions that coursed through us. There were other gatherings, during which we would dream together of the day when we would arrive at the gates of our Holy Land as free women.

There were also regular dark nights when we would talk after work, as we lay on our bunks. Each one spoke of her past, her far-off home and her wonderful Bais Yaakov experiences.

We tried with all our might to keep our spirits up so that we shouldn't fall into despair.

Memories...

"Tell us about your memories, Blum'ke," my friends asked, after sharing their own stories.

I sighed quietly. My memories thundered in my mind; they were alive and fresh. I loved them so dearly, my wonderful sisters, my friends, and teachers. The longing sliced at my heart, and with great difficulty, I controlled myself and began to share some snippets:

Bais Yaakov in Tarnow was all of one big room. Once an hour, the students rotated. First the older ones came to learn, then the younger ones.

After a few years, the Bais Yaakov moved into a bigger building, with three rooms. The higher grades were taught by Morah Basha Leiser, *a"h*, Morah Leika (who was killed with her family during the Holocaust), Morah Carla Stroch-Meiteles, Morah Rivka Englard, Morah Kaufman, Morah Raiza Klingberg, and Mrs. Borenstein, who later lived in Kfar Ata.

Morah Borenstein was a master storyteller. Her stories remained etched in our minds forever. With great vitality, she wove the events until it seemed to me that I was experiencing them in real time. We listened to the stories avidly, wrote them down, and then shared them with anyone willing to listen.

The objective of Bais Yaakov was clear: to save the girls of

Tarnow from the hostile winds that had already ensnared so many. Socialism, in particular, had trapped many young Jews and sacrificed them on the altar of heresy. The point was to instill Yiddishkeit and Jewish pride into the girls, so that we should love Torah and appreciate Torah lives, and rejoice in our status as *Bnos Yisrael*!

The teachers told us riveting stories about Jews throughout the generations who valued Torah and living a life according to Torah. The teachers performed skits for us whenever they could: Chanukah, Tu B'Shevat, Purim.

They wrote the scripts themselves, because we had no books on which to base them. My sister Necha was very talented— she composed rhymes easily, and she wrote wonderful scripts. Raizel, the oldest, was a gifted speaker, and as a young child I would listen to her with baited breath as she spoke passionately about the Chashmonaim.

Raizel succeeded in capturing the hearts of all the girls, who listened to her openmouthed. Chaya also contributed her talents to Bais Yaakov—she wrote beautifully and had a phenomenal memory, and was the live wire of the Bnos group. She wrote scripts and essays on such a high level that she would have been able to compete with experienced journalists. In my opinion, her work could have been published in books.

In the merit of the talents that my family was gifted with from Above, and being intelligent, bright girls, we were very popular in Bais Yaakov. Even though we didn't have particularly nice clothes, nor were we wealthy, the Strom girls enjoyed a strong social status both in Bais Yaakov and in the Polish school.

We learned in Bais Yaakov until the age of fourteen. We were then supposed to continue our studies at the local high school, but our parents were afraid to send us there. There were evil winds blowing in the street; youngsters were tempted and swept up, and our parents were afraid that their daughters would stray from the Jewish path.

There was another reason: many parents didn't send their children to high school because of the steep tuition fees. As an alternative, we studied in private "courses."

Polish girls at the time were not interested in housework, such as they were in Hungary, for example; they liked to read a lot, to become educated, and because of this desire to know so much, many strayed from the path. Girls from the finest homes, whose fathers were tremendous *talmidei chachamim* and whose brothers were *chassidishe bochurim*, fell like ripe fruit into the hands of the Zionist or Socialist movements.

At Bais Yaakov, the teachers worked to instill in our hearts the recognition of the fact that we had to rejoice with our Yiddishkeit; that we shouldn't capitulate and follow the Zionist and Socialist cultures; that we recognized our place and our goal—to become fulfilled, happy Jewish mothers. We were few, but we were proud.

Often, we encountered girls who had already strayed. They tried to argue with us, to explain to us what a "wonderful" world had opened up to them. But the teachers warned us not to get into any arguments, but just to reply, "Look how we are dressed! Don't you see that we are different from you?! We don't belong to you, but to Bais Yaakov and Bnos, and we have nothing to do with you."

Bnos was a movement for *frum* girls who had finished their elementary school education. Under the auspices of Bnos, we gathered each evening at seven o'clock, and heard a *shiur* in Yahadus, in Tehillim, on the *parashah* or various other interesting subjects. Sometimes we read from the *Bais Yaakov Journal*, which had beautiful songs, stories of *tzaddikim* and articles about our rich history.

Sarah Schenirer was admired and respected by all; she was our true leader.

On Shabbos, we gathered to *daven* together, and spent the afternoon hours until *Havdalah* together. On summer *Shabbasos* we went out for long walks.

We constantly remembered to preserve our uniqueness. We didn't go to places that did not suit us, and kept to our principles wherever we were.

Almost all the girls who belonged to Bais Yaakov came from solid, chassidic homes. Only in the lower grades of Bais Yaakov could you find girls from weaker homes, whose fathers were simple Jews, mostly laborers and craftsmen. There were parents who wanted their girls to know how to *daven* and write a Jewish word, to know the history of Am Yisrael and to have basic Jewish knowledge. By contrast, there were homes that got so swept up in the winds of the time that their girls did not step into Bais Yaakov. Bnos was a true salvation and a tremendous spiritual influence on *frum* teenage girls in Poland. They spent many years in the Bnos framework, because in Poland it was not accepted to marry before the age of twenty-four.

When a girl turned eighteen, she traveled to Krakow to study in the seminary for two years. These studies cost a fortune, about one hundred zlotys a month, and not everyone was able to afford it; thus, Bnos was an excellent alternative for the girls who could not attend the seminary.

In the summer we traveled to resort villages, where we spent time together and heard countless *shiurim* from our teachers. Far from the hustle and bustle of the city, in the grassy meadows and forests, with the birds chirping in the background, they infused us with invaluable Jewish values. I also attended camp once, and it remained etched in my memory as one of the most enjoyable experiences I ever had.

For me, it was a beautiful time; I spent so many enjoyable hours in Bnos. Those pleasant memories remained with me always.

Did we imagine during our sweet childhood years what would befall us in the future?!

We didn't dream that all that we had learned, absorbed and experienced in Bais Yaakov and Bnos would accompany us deep into the black years, and would give us tremendous strength; strength we never dreamed we would ever need.

I finished recounting my memories.

Outside, the wind howled, seeking cracks from which to penetrate into the barracks. It wailed sadly instead of me. My anguish was too deep and too great to be expressed in mere tears.

I tried to banish the painful thoughts and looked around me. There was a lonely, sad woman with us, who we tried to get into conversation with to lift her spirits a little at the end of the workday. There were friends who taught other ones English. We knew that we would be liberated by the Americans or the British, and it would be worthwhile to know a bit of English. Some of the prisoners were ready to give up some of their already meager rations as payment for English lessons!

The positive atmosphere that enveloped me in Leipzig, despite the dangerous work, was far preferable to the despair I was surrounded with in Skarzysko.

We had hope. Women who worked in other factories told us that their supervisors sometimes updated them on the political news. At the time, the Germans sensed that their downfall was imminent. They were afraid of the revenge of the Jews, and therefore began to treat them slightly better. On rare occasions, they would—for no apparent reason—give a Jewish prisoner a slice of bread smeared with butter.

The news continued to spread from mouth to ear. We

strengthened each other with the hope that perhaps, we might yet survive until the long awaited liberation.

The food situation in the camp was rapidly deteriorating. They began to serve us foul tasting soup made from *pasternak*, a bitter vegetable normally used to feed cows. The winter had been harsh and the vegetables had been damaged by the freezing temperatures. Often, plates of soup remained full on the table; we simply could not bring ourselves to eat it.

After some time, transports arrived with prisoners from Auschwitz. Already accustomed to starvation, the vile tasting soup was for them royal fare.

Once again I saw how there was no limit to their evil. There are countless rungs on the ladder of troubles. The soup that tasted like poison to us was consumed happily by the starving Yidden from Auschwitz.

The tiny food rations that we were given caused us to obsess constantly about food. There were varying opinions among the prisoners regarding the best way to eat the bread. Some believed it should be eaten all at once, so that they should feel sated for at least a few minutes.

Others claimed, "What will we gain if we become satisfied now but then starve the rest of the day, and become weaker and more malnourished?! It's better to divide the bread into portions!"

I belonged to the group that divided the bread. As such, I felt hungry all day long.

Because of the oppressive hunger, I tried to remain silent. The less I spoke, the more energy I was able to conserve.

17

A Glimmer of Light

I t's remarkable how suddenly a person can change, to trans-
form from a pleasant, kind person to a cruel, heartless one.
That's what happened to the Polish doctor.

While I was in the camp, the doctor treated me devotedly; she
drained the pus from my infected wounds and bandaged them.
She, and the Ukrainian doctor, thought that I was Polish because of
my very light hair and blue eyes. They never asked me my identity
and I received excellent care and kind treatment from them.

Anyone who came to the camp clinic received treatment.
There was just one limitation: one was not allowed to be ill for
more than two weeks, or to come to the clinic too often. In such
cases, the doctors would report to their supervisors, and the
patients were sent to a place from which there was no return.

One day, the order was issued: Anyone who came to the
clinic had to report which block she belonged to. That's how the
doctors knew if the patient was Jewish or gentile.

When I came again to treat my oozing sores, they asked me which block I was from.

"Block 17," I replied.

All at once, anger flared in the eyes of the Polish doctor, certain that I had been trying to trick her. Until then, thinking that I was Polish, she had given me good care and treated me well. Now she discovered that she had been carefully applying iodine and bandages for a Jew!

"You and your kind killed our lord..." she hissed icily. "Get out of here—*gei dir shoin.*"

I felt the insult sear at my heart, and I stopped going to the clinic from that point on. I tried to manage myself, and Ida, my dear friend, would press on the wounds to release the pus.

Sometimes I went to the cellar to drain the pus under a stream of hot water. We were permitted to shower there, unlike in the previous camp, and there were hot water taps in the cellar for showering. We, the prisoners who worked with the galvanized iron, brought industrial laundry soap from the factory and used it to clean ourselves.

The pus would drain under the stream, but I didn't have a scrap of fabric or cotton with which to bandage the wounds.

I found a way to overcome this problem as well. Near where we worked was a huge factory. People were often seriously injured there; fingers were cut off and limbs were gashed with alarming regularity. The wounded were given a piece of cotton and a bandage with which to stanch the bleeding.

I would lie in wait for the opportunity to grab the box into which the remnant scraps fell and use them to bandage my own sores.

We spent nine months at the camp in Leipzig. We Bais Yaakov girls spent as much time together as possible. Each one of us found a good friend, and we all united together. This unity sweetened our bitter lives a bit.

"The Appeal"

The Allied forces drew closer to the front, and the thunder of the bombardments made Europe tremble. The front moved closer to our camp in Leipzig. Each time there was an air raid, we would go down into bomb shelters. Sometimes it happened during work; other times the raids caught us in the camp, during the day or night.

The air raids would continue for two or three hours. When it was during work time we were happy for the break, and would doze off; that's how weak we were.

One day, there was an especially long and intense bombardment. We sat in the shelter for a long time, and when we emerged, we were very sleepy. And then the horrific tragedy occurred to Tamara...

As mentioned, we covered our hands in long gloves that protected us from the chemical substances. And while Tamara was doddering sleepily after emerging from the bomb shelter, she didn't notice that the gears of the machine had caught her glove, together with her hand—Tamara's arm got caught into the machine and was cut off at the shoulder.

Tamara fainted from the searing agony.

A non-Jewish Russian woman who worked alongside her— who was evil and heartless—grasped the hand and tossed it into the machine calling, "Tamara, here is your hand."

The worst thing was that no one cared. No one thought to try and help poor Tamara, laying in a faint on the floor, and losing blood. Almost no one noticed.

In our times, with advanced medical technology, they would have likely sewn Tamara's arm back on and restored this vital limb to her. But in those days, such medical options were not yet available, not to mention that in the camp, no one dreamed of helping Tamara.

In Leipzig, they didn't kill the patients immediately; they took them first to Ravensbrueck. Tamara wasn't transferred because the rail tracks had been bombed. She was "lucky" enough to be taken back to the camp clinic, but her life became even more wretched. Without her right hand, she could not eat, wash herself, or do much of anything. The brutes did not let us help her, forcing us to go out to work. But *HaKadosh Baruch Hu* sent Tamara an angel of rescue in the form of a wonderful girl (who ultimately settled in Bnei Brak) with a noble soul and kind heart who devoted herself completely to Tamara. Each day after work, she sneaked into Tamara's room, putting her own life in danger and ignoring the risk of punishment or death if she was caught.

She cut a piece of fabric from her own dress and sewed a garment as a bribe for the doctor so she would look the other way and let her sit with Tamara. She would spend the time feeding her, combing her hair, and doing whatever she could for her.

One day, that girl said to us, "I'm trying to help Tamara but it's not enough! She's very weak; she lost so much blood! We have to do something for her."

All the Jewish girls decided that that we were going to launch a "food appeal" for Tamara.

It's important for you to understand, dear readers—

Let's say today, an appeal would be held for a needy Jew, and one of the donors would offer to give one million dollars. It's a huge amount, but it doesn't even compare to the sacrifice we made then, when we donated our already paltry portion of food. Women and girls agreed willingly to spare a few crumbs of their own bread for poor Tamara. We gave her our last crumbs of life! We put ourselves at such risk; we could have easily died of hunger.

A lot of food was collected during the appeal, and then a

problem arose: Where would we hide the food? We were not allowed to store any food. In the end we found a solution, and Tamara was able to eat fuller rations to help revive her weakened body.

Again, the beauty of the Jewish soul was revealed! *Di sheinkeit fun di Yiddishe neshamah!* Again we proved that the more the evildoers battered and depressed our bodies, they could not destroy our souls. They were unable to erase the *tzelem Elokim* no matter how hard they tried.

That is how we Jews are. The Creator formed us in such a way that even in the most difficult situations, the Jewish sense of compassion hidden deep, bursts forth the moment it is called upon.

Pesach 5705/1945 was drawing closer. We were very close to liberation but still in bondage.

One girl tried to escape the camp and was caught. She was hanged publicly, in front of all the inmates. The girl walked to her death with her head held high.

Meanwhile, we were finally transferred from the dangerous iron galvanizing factory to an aluminum factory. The work conditions were considerably easier.

Beside me sat a heretic from Vilna who constantly grumbled and cursed. "It's only because of the Jews that I was sent to the camps!" she claimed. The Germans, *ym"s,* checked into the origins of every person, even if they were heretics, and thoroughly researched if they or one of their ancestors—four generations back—were of Jewish extraction.

These apostates suffered just like we did. One of them, a refined person, lamented over the fact that her parents had given up their religion. "Why am I to blame?" she sighed. But the one who sat next to me was just malicious. Despite her personal suffering, she was happy that "all the Jews were suffering."

On the other side of me sat my friend Ida. The work we were doing was inestimably easier than what we had been doing at the previous factory. We had to count and sort pieces of aluminum, and so, while sitting together, we tried to remember the *Aseres Hadibros*. What was the first one, what was the second one… We challenged ourselves and exerted our brains so our senses wouldn't atrophy completely from lack of use.

Our gatherings with the Rebbetzin in the cellar also infused us with the strength to keep our spirits up in those waning hours.

An Unattainable Dream

In the Leipzig camp, poor, starving Rosa lost her hundred dollars.

Rosa, who had been deported from Germany to Poland, was afraid to speak German. She was very dependent on the Polish girls and turned to me for help.

Despite all the *selektions* and thorough inspections that we had undergone in all the camps, there were prisoners among us who had succeeded in smuggling valuables into the camp. Rosa was one of them. She had smuggled in one hundred dollars, which she had sewn into a hidden hem in her clothes. She had been thoroughly inspected, but no one had found her money. She would buy candies and distribute them to all of us, as I mentioned earlier.

Rosa suffered terribly from hunger. Often I thought that she reminded me, *l'havdil*, of a starving dog dashing to and fro, smelling and sniffing after food.

On one of the especially hungry days, Rosa turned to me: "Why do I have to hold on to my money? I can ask one of the gentiles who works with us to bring me bread for the money. Speak to him, Blumke!" she asked me.

According to camp laws, we were not allowed to accumulate bread under any circumstances. But we were so hungry, we couldn't think of anything else. When we went to work, I approached the gentile together with Rosa and proposed the deal: one hundred dollars for bread.

"Okay," the gentile agreed. "I'll give you thirty loaves."

That night, after work, Rosa asked me: "Blumka, how will we get the bread into the camp?"

"Ask the gentile to bring one loaf each day. We'll cut it into pieces and take it with us."

The next day, after work, she ran to the gentile to ask for the bread. "Who said anything about thirty loaves?" the gentile declared. "I will only give you twenty-five!"

"I'll get back to you tomorrow," Rosa said. That night Rosa came to tell me what the gentile had said.

"Grab those twenty-five loaves!" I urged her. "Who knows how much he will deduct the longer we wait."

"Okay," she told me. "I will."

The next day, she went over to the man and said, "I've decided to buy twenty-five loaves from you. Give them to me."

"No, no," the gentile replied now. "Today, I won't give you twenty-five—only twenty!"

Rosa replied that she would think about it and tell him the next day what she had decided.

She felt bad about the ten loves she had lost. She wanted to think about whether it was worth it to give one hundred dollars—which she had risked her life to guard against detection—to the gentile for twenty loaves of bread.

That night, Rosa came to me again and whispered her painful secret: "Now he only wants to give me twenty breads."

I felt the pressure for her, and urged her, "Grab the twenty he is offering!"

But the next day, the gentile disappointed her again by offering only ten loaves. "You know that during wartime there is a shortage and the bread is running out. It's almost impossible to obtain!"

"Run and take the ten!" I whispered to Rosa when she came to consult with me.

But she thought the gentile was trying to deceive her and refused to give in. If yesterday he could have gotten twenty breads, why couldn't he do the same today?

"Rosa, you're suffering so badly from hunger!" I argued with her. "Run and grab the ten breads he is offering, and you'll have bread for every day, like we said."

But by the time she returned to the gentile to accept the ten, he was only offering five breads.

And that's how the number of loaves steadily decreased, until she said to me dejectedly: "He's not ready to give me more than three breads for my one hundred dollars."

The next day, when we went to work, Rosa was determined to buy the three breads.

That day it was Rosa's turn to sweep the factory floor, which was covered by pieces of aluminum by the end of the day.

At the end of the workday, we had to report to the commander to ensure no one had run away. We were counted twice a day – once at the beginning of the day and once at the end.

Sometimes, there were air raids, and we ran to hide in the bomb shelters. They would count us after we emerged from the shelter to make sure no one had escaped. Once, three Russian prisoners did manage to get away, and the remaining prisoners were forced to stand in front of the commander for an endless amount of time as a punishment.

That day, Rosa came to the commander and began to finger the hidden hem in her clothes...

To her indescribable horror, she did not feel the money.

"Oh, no! No! It's not here," she whispered to me in anguish. "*Ich hob ess farloiren*, I lost it..." she whispered in German.

"Rosa, run back," I whispered to her.

She raced back to work and searched for the money. She returned after some time, red-eyed. "*Leider*, that's it. The money is gone," she wept.

And that's how the dream of her loaves of bread was buried, and Rosa remained so very hungry...

Rosa survived the war, *baruch Hashem*, and came to Eretz Yisrael. Her sister also survived and they met up in the DP camps. Rosa married a Jew from Warsaw and had one daughter. Her sister settled in Tel Aviv.

Rosa's sad story always reminds me of the *churban*, and the story cited in *Chazal* about Marsa bas Beisus, who was very wealthy, and sent her servant to the store over and over again, until all the different kinds of bread were sold out.

Each time I read this story in the Midrash, the memory of Rosa and her bread rises vividly in my mind.

18

HALACHIC STRINGENCIES AT THE THRESHOLD OF DEATH

Would the beasts let us live until the moment we so yearned for, the moment of liberation?

We were afraid that they would not! As such, the reports that the end of the war was near did not lift our spirits. We were still being held captive by the strong and well-armed Germans. Had they wanted to, they could have easily shot all of us. We were so weak we could hardly stand.

They didn't send us to work anymore; the Germans no longer needed the increased production we provided. Their defeat was inevitable, so they decided to send us on the Death March.

The Germans could not come to terms with the fact that we would be liberated from the camps by their enemies, the Russians or the Americans, and wanted us to die on our own on this exhausting journey.

It was nighttime when we were ordered to prepare to leave.

"Formations of five!" they thundered at us. I made sure to stand near my close friends.

The Germans gave us "food for the way": A slice of bread and some other measly food item. None of us imagined that this was supposed to last us for three weeks!

We set out exhausted, drained, and worried before we even began. Where were we being taken? What would our end be? It was very frightening.

The sick women and girls remained in the camps; the Germans did not want them to slow us down. They concealed explosives all over the camp and left the camp, together with us. A few hours later, the entire camp exploded and the buildings collapsed. I heard about this afterwards from women who had remained behind and survived this as well.

Among the ruins lay a woman who miraculously survived. She was from Beitsch in Poland, and had belonged to Bnos Agudas Yisrael in her youth. Through Bnos, she got to know my oldest sister, Raizel, *Hy"d*.

After the war, I was staying at the Sternbuch home in Switzerland. On Simchas Torah, many survivors who had been invited for the *chag* stayed in the house. Among the guests, I noticed that woman, and beside her—remarkably—a sweet, charming, smart little girl. People said that the mother and child were about to leave Switzerland for Canada after Switzerland refused to allow war refugees to remain in the country.

I did not recognize her at first, but when we spoke at the Sternbuchs I asked which camp she had been in and where she was from. That is how I found out that we had been in the Leipzig camp together.

She told me she had been deported with her husband to the Skarzysko camp in Poland, then alone to Leipzig. I asked her how she had managed to survive the terrible hunger. "I always had a small bottle of water with me, which I kept hidden," she told me. "When I felt the hunger pangs, I sipped the water a bit."

When we set out on the Death March, she remained in the camp of her own free will, pretending to be sick. When the building exploded, she fell and lay between the broken walls and shattered glass. Just then, alone in the glass and stones, her daughter was born.

A few minutes after that, the Allied forces reached the camp. They took mother and baby to the hospital, and that's how they were decreed to live.

It was a tremendous miracle, *Hashgachah pratis* that proved that when a person is destined to live or be born—it can happen even amid utter chaos.

Unforgivable Apathy

Long rows of emaciated, weary people marched on the roads, escorted by the German guards who kept us under close watch. Our wooden shoes dragged on the ground, creating a morose staccato.

We walked and walked and walked, passing tranquil villages, flowering fields, and forests that emitted a heady aroma. The walking was constant, with no clear destination, and we felt like we were trudging through a grey fog.

We marched in organized rows. Anyone who deviated even slightly was shot on the spot. Girls collapsed on the side of the road, spent, and were shot. Only a quarter of us survived that dreadful march.

The Allied forces bombarded often. During an attack, we slowed our pace and hid behind a fence or wall.

The bombarding planes sometimes flew so low that we could see if they were American, Russian, or British. The pilots were also able to discern the people on the ground, and would direct their ammunition towards the German soldiers. Our escorts tried to mask their identities in order to be spared the bombardments. SS soldiers who feared for their lives took off their hats and insignias.

Once, during a bombardment, we were standing behind a wall in a German city. We were abysmally tired and weary, and the gunfire was raging above us. A few of us were barefoot, while others wore torn, threadbare shoes.

This terrible scene touched the heart of a German who passed us and he looked at us and said, "*Unzere eibige shanda*, our eternal shame." That was the only time we heard an expression of remorse or shame from a German.

Aside for that isolated remark, we never saw a shred of compassion from the German civilians. They gazed at us as though we had arrived from another planet; they saw us dying but never gave us a morsel of food.

We would wander through forests or drop to the ground in the fields because of the air raids. We sometimes lay for hours until it passed.

We were in the heart of a flaming battlefield! Above our heads, the fire of war burned, and we marched between the shells and flying bullets. Often, bombs fell around us but did not explode.

The fire burned on the outside, and inside our tortured bodies, we were being eaten up by hunger. For three weeks, we were hardly given a thing to eat!

We plucked grass from the wayside and sucked the roots, the tiny bit of sweetness we gleaned momentarily reviving us. We also picked unripe kohlrabies that peeked out from the ground, and ate them.

Discussions

In the depths of despair and the valley of death, where humanity had sunk to its lowest point and had nearly been eradicated from the face of Europe; during endless marches between forests and fields, from bombs to shells—we *frum* girls in the group found time to meet and discuss the pressing issues of the hour with the Rebbetzin.

One of the significant questions that arose during the Death March was:

"Let's say I have one drop of water and my friend is literally fainting. I feel that I am also going to faint soon. Do I have to give the bit of water I have left to my friend, or may I save it for myself so that I won't faint?"

The question itself proves the power of a positive surrounding and the solidarity of a high quality group. In the merit of our togetherness, even in those circumstances, in the chaos, lack of values and humanity, we were able to think like people with emotions, to discuss things in a Jewish way. We were able to think of others and not wallow entirely in selfishness; we left a small corner in our minds for thinking of others and considering what *halachah* demanded of us...

All this stemmed from a pure desire that burned within us the entire time to do the will of Hashem as much as possible, to rise above the existing reality and cling tenaciously to our values.

The journey wore on... Starving and weak, we marched through fields; beside me, girls fainted and collapsed one after the other. One day, I noticed that Ida, my dear friend, had collapsed. She could no longer forge on.

Not Ida! How devoted she was to me! I could not bear the thought that she would die now, and would remain laying there unburied...

Just then, we passed a German town and stopped for an air raid. From afar, I suddenly saw a well; I ran towards it quickly and drew water into a small container I had with me. I ran back to Ida and attempted to revive her while dripping drops of life-giving water into her mouth. She awoke, but refused to continue walking.

That was it; the suffering had won out. She had lost the will to live. There were many others like her, who, drained and exhausted by the battle to survive, upon reaching the limit of their endurance, decided: "No more!" They just could not go on—and gave up on living in those final moments before the liberation.

I didn't want Ida to die! My heart ached...Ida was such a good girl, and had helped me so much in our travails through the camps...Soon, light would break through into the darkness; we would be liberated. She just couldn't die now!

"Ida, dear Ida, you have to be strong!" I pleaded with her, and spoke words of encouragement into her ear. "Your brothers are waiting for you in Eretz Yisrael, Ida'le! You will live, you will yet meet them in Eretz Yisrael. Ida, do me a favor, get up and we'll continue..."

Suddenly, I felt a blow to my hand. It was the evil SS woman! The container in my hand tipped over and the precious water poured out...

Although I had no more water, the few drops I had managed to drip into Ida's mouth had aroused her from her faint and she agreed to get up and forge on.

Ida was terribly starved and could not suffer any more. I ran to the kohlrabi field we had discovered, and grabbed a bunch of branches. I wanted to give them to Ida, but that evil SS woman was determined to keep us under her iron grip. She fired her weapon into the air so that I wouldn't dare eat the kohlrabi or feed it to anyone else.

We were starving, starving, starving! Our stomachs growled, pleading for bread; our insides clenched with hunger. We saw the local Germans hiding sliced potatoes in the ground and the minute they turned their backs we tried to dig up the potatoes from the ground, but the wicked German officers didn't let us. I remember one of them, a fat, nasty woman. She held her gun in both hands and fired at whoever she thought was heading in the direction of the potatoes.

Where Is the Rice?

"That's it! We're staying here. We can't go on," we informed the Germans. We really couldn't. Our legs refused to carry us any further. "If we don't get food, we won't be able to walk anymore."

So they gave us…raw rice. "They sent it to you from the Red Cross," they told us.

But how can one eat hard, raw rice?!

Fortunately, the air raids started up again and we had to stop our interminable march. We sat near a forest and thought of ways to make the rice edible.

Among us were Ukrainian prisoners who were feeling very confident. The Russian planes were flying very low and they tossed out leaflets with words of encouragement for the Ukrainians: "Be strong, we are coming to liberate you!" There were also rumors that the pilots had tossed biscuits out of the planes.

The Ukrainians dared to ask the female German officers permission to kindle a fire, and they got it. They pulled branches from a tree and lit them to be able to cook the rice. In what, you may ask? From water that they extracted from the mud that was on the ground.

I approached one Ukrainian and asked if I could put a tin with my rice on her fire.

"No," she replied, "unless you give me half of your rice."

I refused. *I won't give it to her,* I resolved. *Maybe tomorrow I'll gain access to fire and will be able to cook the precious rice. It's a shame on the half portion.*

And that's how we went to sleep on the damp ground, starving. The snow was a pillow for our heads. I hid my bit of rice in a bottle-like container beneath my head.

But the next morning, I could not find the rice. The Ukrainian remembered that I hadn't eaten mine, and while I slept she stole it from me.

That's how I spared myself from having to find a way to cook the rice—and remained starving, starving, starving...

We plucked the prickly leaves from the ground, and called them *di shtechediker bletter,* the sharp leaves, and ate them.

And we continued to starve. It was miraculous how long we were able to hold out without succumbing to starvation.

The Revolt

The Sudetenland was the last part of Europe to be liberated from the Germans, and that's where we were marching with our camp commanders.

The region was surrounded on all sides. On one side were the Allies and on the other, the Russian Army. The land under German control shrank steadily each day and the Germans led us in hysteria, from here to there and there to here, trying to distance themselves from the battlefront, but to no avail. During the flight, we crossed the Bug River several times, back and forth.

The guards sensed the noose tightening around their necks and didn't know what to do with us. Contact with their superiors was spotty and without orders from the higher-ups they didn't want to decide on our fate on their own.

Releasing us was out of the question. They couldn't bear the thought that their Final Solution would not come to fruition.

They marched alongside us and watched over us, as they protected themselves using various tactics. They walked instead of riding in vehicles for fear that the enemy aircraft or tanks would identify them. They preferred to march with us to the American front, because if they fell prisoner to the Russians, the latter would destroy them completely.

Our camp was comprised only of women, but male prisoners from other camps joined us en route. Throughout the marches, there were people who had escaped or who had been liberated before us, but it was a tremendous risk. Anyone who tried to escape was shot.

Many, many people lost their lives on the Death March, and remained sprawled on the ground where they fell, on the road, in the fields, or in the forests. They were mostly men. The Gemara says that men find the strain of traveling more difficult than women. One day, I saw a man hugging a thick tree trunk, and thus, standing in that position, he stopped breathing. There were many others like him.

One day, we decided to revolt. "We cannot go further without food," we said.

We stopped and refused to go any further. The Germans, sensing their end was near and fearing for their lives, stopped with us in the town of Olga-Wicz. They entered the villagers' homes and ordered them to cook potatoes in their peels for us. Each person received *one* potato after three weeks of wandering and starving!

We collapsed onto the floor of a silo and sat on the straw as we slowly ate our potatoes, but then… we couldn't get up.

Our machines had stopped working and refused to start up again. Our bodies, which had worked and worked and worked, walking endlessly, could no longer move. We just couldn't!!

The Germans began to howl at us madly: "*Veiter*! Get moving! Up, now!!"

But none of us rose. "Whatever happens, happens," we told ourselves. "Let them do what they want—let them kill us. We can't walk anymore. We are not continuing. It's just not possible."

The Germans were wild with fury. "We'll shoot all of you like dogs!" they screamed, but to no avail; we did not move.

A few of the "older" women, around age forty, who were afraid, heaved themselves up and continued to walk. They had gone just a few meters when we heard the shots break the quiet. They had shot those poor women. Apparently, that's what they had planned to do to all of us.

Before they left, the Germans didn't forget to lock us in the silo. We remained there while the Germans continued their flight.

We sat helplessly, weak and exhausted, and barely breathing. A few hours passed, and then night fell.

We didn't know what was happening but just being able to rest was a tremendous relief. Outside, rain fell, and we listened to the steady patter of the drops, sheltered by the roof of the silo.

Outside, the bombs shrieked and exploded; the battlefront was drawing ever closer to the village we were in, which was very close to Berlin, the capital of Germany and the heart of the battleground.

19

FROM THE FRYING PAN INTO THE FIRE

We sat listlessly, exhausted. Our starved brains were hollow and bare of thoughts.

Suddenly we heard footsteps.

"The Germans are gone! The Russians are here! Everything is over!" we heard cries in Polish.

A Polish gentile who had come to Germany to earn a livelihood was the one who brought us the news of our liberation. He pulled away the slats of wood that had locked the silo and opened the doors wide.

Silence reigned. The trumpets of war had stilled; the town of Olga-Wicz was calm and tranquil, as though no shells and bombs had been flying over it just a few hours ago.

Now that we were finally free to go, we couldn't. We didn't have the strength to pull ourselves up from the ground. The world seemed to stand still.

In the end, a few brave girls dared to creep outside. They knocked on the doors of the village homes. "We want you to cook us potatoes again," they demanded. "Not one, a few per person."

The Germans residents were stocked with a tremendous supply of food that would have sufficed for several years, and were certainly in a position to give us what we asked for.

The girls went to the barn and demanded that the cows be milked so we could have some milk. They also entered empty apartments that the Germans had abandoned, and searched for food there. The Germans were terrified of the Russians and what they would do to them. They were less afraid of the British and the Americans. The area where we were was captured by the Russians, and many civilians fled for their lives.

In the empty apartments, the women found an abundance of bread, marmalade, and other foodstuffs. I didn't go. I didn't have the energy. I sat or lay with my friends in the silo and the lice crawled all over us and bit us…We hadn't showered for three or four weeks, we hadn't changed clothes, we'd been sleeping on the ground, and now we were suffering unpleasant side effects.

One day, a Russian patrol came. "Now, we Russians rule this area and we will transfer you to the other side of the border," they announced.

The Czech prisoners among us were sent back to Czechoslovakia right away, while we, the Jews, remained in the village, almost lifeless.

"You're very weak and neglected," the Russian patrollers said. "And that's why we, the new rulers here, will divide you among the local farmers, where you will eat and regain your strength."

We looked like shadows of our former selves. We could barely drag ourselves to the homes we were assigned to.

They divided us into groups of five to seven girls. Ida and I were assigned to the home of a very nasty German woman. Our lives in her company were not worth living. She would prevent us from coming into the house and made us sleep in the storage room. The room was between two floors and filled with straw. The German woman locked us in and let us out only to eat.

Other women did receive good food and ate heartily, but they suffered terribly as a result. Their shrunken stomachs were not able to handle all the food and it caused them great pain. Many of the liberated prisoners died right afterwards from the sudden inundation of normal food, which literally killed them.

I, by contrast, could not eat at all. My appetite was totally suppressed, so I asked the farmwoman, "Please can I have a pickle to stimulate my appetite?"

"I don't have any," she lied brazenly. She refused to fulfill even this small request.

Later, when the Russians soldiers came to the village, we saw her hiding barrels full of pickles and brandy in the ground in her field. The villagers there had everything, but they hid it for themselves, leaving very little for us.

Two or three days later, Berlin was captured. The war was finally over.

The village of Olga-Wicz was not far from Berlin. One clear day, a vehicle with Russian soldiers drunk with victory, drove into the town. These were the famed heroes who had liberated Berlin, the capital city.

They were horrifically arrogant, and acted like they owned the world, and that everyone had to bow to them because they had captured Berlin!

The soldiers were hungry and thirsty. They demanded that the tenants give them brandy, and anything else their hearts desired. They stormed into the homes and caused damage, spilling sacks of flour and the like. They roared, cheered, and pillaged for the fun of it, in their drunken victory rampage.

We had no pity on the Germans and were rather smug at this small victory. "Our" farm lady was especially punished: the "heroes" shot her husband, claiming he had served in the German army. Initially, she cried and mourned over her husband's death, but then she seemed to forget about it and found comfort in her son.

The Dangerous Russians

The wild Russians took up residence in the apartments above the home of the landlady. They were Mongols, central Asians, with slanted eyes and stocky builds, and it was very dangerous to be around them.

They demanded that we sit at the same table with them, and drink brandy with them from tea glasses, like they were used to. Despite their being our liberators, these were no friends of ours. They were extremely dangerous, and made it clear to us in Russian—which is similar to Polish—that, "we liberated you and you have to pay us back for that." We were terrified that they would not even leave us alive in the end. We decided that we had to hide. Girls fled to the gentile cemetery while others hid in cupboards and behind doors. At the time, some of us remembered stories we had heard from our mothers about what had happened during World War I. The Russians had invaded Poland and caused havoc among Jewish families. Now, too, we were afraid of our fate in the hands of the Russians.

At night they arrived, banging on our doors as they called, "Open up, and if not, we will shoot you." We were afraid to open, because they might shoot us all the same.

Those weeks in the German village were almost too difficult to bear. For us, it was almost like another Holocaust…In a sense, it was worse. During the war, the fiends did what they wanted with us, but here, we had to constantly come up with ways to evade the dangerous Russians, because if we didn't meet their demands—they would shoot.

Five survivors, dear, pious Bais Yaakov girls (among them Schechter from Krakow), were attacked by the Russians. The girls gave up their lives *al kiddush Hashem* as the Russians shot them to death. How horrific, how dreadful! Girls who had gone through the horrors of the war, survived, and could have established future generations… May Hashem remember them for good, because they gave their lives to sanctify His Name.

One day, the Russians came to the storage room where we slept. They passed by an older woman who sat with her sixteen-year-old daughter. The "older" woman was all of about forty, but her hair was already white and she seemed far older than that. The Russians left the mother and daughter alone, and did not harass them, going up to the next floor.

I ran with Ida to the top floor. We buried ourselves deep in the straw. The soldiers raced around as if possessed. First, they went to the German landlady and then they came up to us. They began to rummage in the straw with the butts of their guns; suddenly, I felt a butt touch me, and it got stuck in my thick heel…

I have already told you about the "bonuses" that I used to buy the wooden clogs. The butt of the gun got stuck in the heel of the clog; I began to tremble. I *davened* in my heart, *Ribbono shel Olam, in the labor camps and the concentration camps, You guarded me constantly, and ultimately, I merited the liberation. Will my end come now?! Give me an idea, Merciful Father, what should I do now to save myself?!*

I was afraid even to breathe, lest the straw rise and fall…and then Hashem gave me a good idea. I took my foot out of the shoe and burrowed further into the straw, but the shoe remained where it was. The soldier thought his gun had hit a stray piece of wood and turned to go...

I remained hiding there.

My friend Ida did not have such a shoe, nor an idea like I did. She was discovered. She didn't even know Russian well. Now, after surviving the Holocaust, she had fallen prey to the Russians...

These were the kind of times we experienced.

A few weeks later, we discovered several Jewish officers among the Russians, and we asked for their assistance. They assigned a guard for each apartment, but that didn't always help either.

At that point, the gentile woman allowed me to move into her living quarters.

We completely lost track of the days. Where were we up to in the Jewish calendar? Was it before or after Pesach?

One day, Jews passed us and said, "According to our calculations, it's Pesach now."

We were surprised. We thought that Pesach had taken place while we were still in the camp. Indeed, it had. But it was no wonder that there were Jews who had made a mistake in their calculations under those circumstances.

20

ON THE ROOF OF THE TRAIN

T ears streamed down the faces of the American soldiers. A horrific encounter awaited them when they liberated the camps; they came face to face with the depths of the brutality, with the wretched remnants of man and the lifeless shadows. They brought doctors to try and heal the prisoners and to set them back on the path of the living.

We had a different fate in store. The Russians who liberated us were merciless and saw no need to worry about us. On the contrary, they sent us "home."

The foreign subjects who were not German citizens were ordered to return to their native lands. "Enough with the vacation, the war is over, you've rested enough!" they jeered, and sent us on our way.

And that's how our stay at the German "hotel" ended.

We survivors had not yet managed to activate our ability to think for ourselves, so when everyone was returning to Poland we set out to do the same.

This opened a new chapter in my life, a journey that was both difficult and very dangerous.

We sat on the exposed roofs of train cars that carried coal, without any covering or blanket, and rode and rode and rode.

It was a dreadful experience. It was physically difficult and spiritually dangerous.

On rare occasions we were able to slip into a carriage and sit inside. Sometimes, there were Jewish soldiers from Russia in these carriages, and they were very curious to hear about our lives. They understood that we were *frum* girls, and often we heard remarks such as, "Yes, my grandmother also lit candles," or, "My grandmother would say that we had to use two separate sinks in the kitchen." But those soldiers, unfortunately, were far from Judaism. We realized that they really had no interest in returning to Russia. They tried to find ways to settle in Poland instead of returning to the Communist "utopia."

We were hungry, but no one worried about us although sometimes those Russian Jewish soldiers brought us food. However, we did try as much as possible to avoid accepting their help.

Shabbos was settling on the cities of battered Germany.

Before Shabbos, we got off the roofs of the train cars and entered a German town. We were able to find a place to stay, but it was a most unpleasant Shabbos. The house was teeming with young German gentiles, who made hateful, anti-Semitic remarks. We saw that they were restraining themselves from voicing their true sentiments, but every so often a comment escaped, revealing their rabid hatred of Jews.

After the nightmarish Shabbos, we continued our dangerous journey in a hostile environment. Once, we fled from one train to another to escape being assaulted; another time, the train wobbled dangerously and we—on the roof–nearly fell to our deaths, but the train eventually steadied and continued on its journey...

After unbelievable travails, we finally reached Krakow. We looked terrible. We still wore our prisoners' uniforms, our eyes were red and burning from the coal, and we were exhausted and skeletally thin. The trip that should have taken eighteen hours took us three weeks, and it had clearly taken a toll, on top of the difficult years we had experienced prior to that.

Rabid Hatred

The war ended on 25 Iyar 5705 (May 8, 1945) and we arrived in Poland some two and a half months after that, in the middle of Av/July. We had spent six weeks in the German village, followed by three weeks of traveling that brought us to Poland.

In Krakow we met a nucleus of a Jewish community comprised of survivors. No one greeted us, and there was no help forthcoming from people who had themselves experienced the horrors. They didn't have what to share with us. There was no food and no one offered us a roof under which we could sleep. That first night, we slept in the street.

After recovering somewhat, I began to search for my aunt, who had lived in Krakow. I knew that she lived there and I could only hope she had survived the war.

Miraculously, I found her! She had survived, together with her daughter, under false identities and forged Aryan papers. Her husband had traveled to Lemberg at the beginning of the war to obtain food for his family, but she hadn't heard anything from him since. She and her daughter had been able to survive.

Throughout the war, my aunt was helped extensively by her gentile servant, who was part German. My aunt disguised herself as a gentile who had come to help the servant, and would walk with her daughter with everyone thinking that the girl was the servant's daughter. After the liberation, the servant came with all kinds of claims: "The child is mine," she told my aunt. "I'm the one who saved her."

My aunt was stunned! Would she lose her daughter now, after they had survived so much? Ultimately, the servant let my aunt pay her a large sum of money, and she was able to keep her daughter.

My aunt was overjoyed to see me! I spent a few weeks in her house but it was not a suitable place for me. My aunt, who had been masquerading as a gentile for the duration of the war, had decided to retain her assumed identity, claiming it was dangerous to be a Jew.

How tragic! Many Jews spent the war hiding under false identities and continue to live as gentiles after the war as well. There was still a fear of non-Jews; the Poles continued to display anti-Semitism even though the war was over.

Once, one of my friends, who had taken on a gentile identity for the war and had false papers, told me that she had been in Lodz on the day of the liberation. In Poland, the mood was joyous; the non-Jewish residents took to the streets and danced with glee at finally being rid of the German oppression.

Suddenly she noticed one of the celebrants leaning over the sidewalk; he was writing something in large white letters: "Finish off the Jews!"

Which Jews did he mean? There was hardly a Jew on the street! The survivors had not yet come back from the camps in Europe, and certainly not from Russia. There were only a handful of Jews who had been liberated before the war was over and they could be seen here and there. But the gentiles were suddenly full of alacrity to express their hatred. There was even a certain

Polish political party, the National Party, whose platform was persecuting Jews!

While traveling on the train from Krakow to Lodz, I heard members of this party speaking virulently of the Jews. My aunt made sure I had a Polish certificate so that they would not harm me during the trip.

On the Kibbutz

While in my aunt's house I heard the news: the Vaad Hatzolah of the *rabbanim* of America, in conjunction with Agudas Yisrael, had established organizations for the survivors, which were called kibbutzim. A kibbutz was established in Tarnow and my fellow survivors, the girls from Tarnow, gathered there. "Come to us, Blumke. Come be with us," they invited me over and over again.

One day, I decided to listen to them and return to Tarnow. The kibbutz there was comprised of a hodgepodge of orphaned refugees, often without siblings as well. On rare occasions, one would see two sisters together.

Kibbutzim for refugees were established in Krakow, Chenstochow, Sosnovtze, Lodz, and other cities.

We decided to try to make up for each other's losses. We united and created a family of devoted "sisters." We did everything together. We slept side by side, ate together, and organized *shiurim* that we all attended.

After the experiences in the camps, each one of us longed for love and warmth, for the knowledge that someone cared, for the taste of devotion that we so lacked.

We tried to encourage and cheer each other up. The atmosphere in the kibbutz was warm and unifying and the time passed pleasantly.

Among the counselors, I remember Shifra Singer, who later became Rebbetzin Yudassin, who had been a teacher in Bais Yaakov before the war. She gave us inspiring *shiurim*. There was also Rena Finkelstein, who was part of Bnos in Krakow before the war.

I became an English teacher. I taught the girls basic English, things that I had learned on my own. It is safe to assume that my students, who later moved to America, know English far better than I do...

There was another kibbutz nearby for men, among them *rabbanim*. One of them was a renowned gaon named Rav Hirsch, *zt"l*, among others.

These Jews had a tremendous task of resurrecting the ruins of the Jewish world and restarting life from scratch. The prisoners who returned from the camps after long periods were completely disconnected from a life of Torah and mitzvos. For many long, difficult years, they hadn't had the opportunity to *daven* and serve Hashem. Therefore, a Jew who *davened* after the war, and who observed kashrus and Shabbos, was considered a total tzaddik.

Regretfully, the war robbed many people of their faith. There were Jews who had been observant before the war, but eventually changed their outlook. The ordeals they endured damaged their faith and robbed them of their senses.

There was also an interesting reverse trend: People who before the war were far from Yiddishkeit drew closer to a life of Torah after the war. Non-religious girls who had gone to the labor and concentration camps met and spent the time there with G-d fearing girls, were surprised to see the kind, humane nature, and refinement of the *frum* girls, and as a result, joined them.

I knew one girl who had studied in the gymnasium before the war. After the Holocaust, she came upon a kibbutz of *frum* girls, and observed our beautiful lives. She absorbed the elevated, unified atmosphere, the mutual encouragement and support, and the efforts to banish despair and to infuse our lives with joy—and she decided to join our circle. She married a Satmar *chassid* and established a beautiful family. There were several other girls like her.

During the frozen winter of 5706/1946, the exiles to Russia returned to Poland. Fractured families had survived the harsh labor in the forests and steppes of Russia, the hunger and the torture. Some of the Yidden who returned from Russian exile remained firm in their faith, while others strayed from the path, to our sorrow.

Organizations and committees tried to help us; most notably we were supported by the Joint. Every so often, they gave us money, which we used to buy ready-made clothing or material to sew clothing in place of the faded rags we had been wearing.

We also helped each other. We felt like we were part of one big family, and there was a harmonious atmosphere. We didn't envy one another, and no one was concerned that someone else had more than she.

One older girl among us was an expert seamstress, and sewed each of us a nice Shabbos outfit. My friend Chana Gelbart succeeded in retrieving her parents' assets. She set aside money to buy a dress for me, and bought a shirt for another friend.

The Trial

One day, we went to order a shirt from a seamstress who lived near the local courthouse. She measured the garment, and as she did, a gentile neighbor burst inside and began to shout, "Oh, you foolish girls, why are you busy with such nonsense?! Go to the courthouse. An interesting trial is taking place..."

We were curious and hurried to the courthouse. It was a prominent trial against the commander of the Jewish police, whose sister had studied with me in Bais Yaakov (Bais Yaakov also had students from homes that were not as religious because the father wanted their daughters to know something about Judaism.)

The defendant was brought to the stand in handcuffs. On one side of him were his sister and his lawyer, and on the other side was the state prosecutor. We sat down and listened to the proceedings, hearing how the man was accused of cruel behavior in the ghetto. They claimed that he would stand at the ghetto gate when the Jewish forced laborers returned from work and beat them mercilessly with his truncheon. He would also stand at the gate that separated Ghetto A from Ghetto B and beat those who passed through.

There were witnesses who testified on his behalf, maintaining that, "the defendant would warn the Jews going to work that the Gestapo was at the gate. He was good to the Jews." The defending counsel argued that there was no reason to bring charges against a young man who had observed endless acts of incitement against the Jews, which galvanized him to harass them. In general, in times of danger, the brain does not work, the lawyer said…He brought an example from French Marshal Philippe Pétain, famed general and lauded hero. He, too, was brought down by Nazi pressure and obeyed their orders. So how could claims be brought against an eighteen-year-old youth who had lost his sound judgment under terrible pressure?!

There were testimonies on both sides, until one woman rose to the witness stand.

She related that during the last deportation from the ghetto to the camp in Plashow, she managed to smuggle her son into the train car. As previously related, the Germans first sent Jewish inspectors to check the trains to make sure that no one had smuggled a child on board, then conducted another inspection to double check.

The defendant entered the rail car, the woman related, and saw the child that she had been holding close, and informed the German officers. They took the child from her and shot him to death. "He is the murderer of my son!" the bereaved mother wept accusingly.

After she finished her testimony, silence reigned in the courtroom. The judges deliberated for five minutes before they issued their terrible verdict: if the defendant had caused the death of a child, he would be punished by death.

When the sister heard the verdict, she fell into a faint. The defendant lowered his head, and boos and catcalls were heard from the audience.

I felt horrible. This trial legitimized pure anti-Semitism!

It was clear as day that the trial had been conducted by the Poles not because they sought justice, but because they had found a suitable opportunity to harass a Jew.

How many Jews had non-Jews killed, directly or indirectly?! It's impossible to count them! Why had the gentile killers not been brought to trial?

As an aside, the judges offered the defendant the opportunity to appeal to the president to ask for clemency. I do not know what happened at the end, or if he was indeed put to death, because at the time, verdicts were carried out quietly, without fanfare, because everyone did as they pleased. There was no accountability whatsoever.

We emerged from the courthouse feeling anguished. Our hearts tore over the fact that the Poles, the tremendous Jew haters, were taking revenge for our blood by killing a Jew for it. Even though we had also sustained beatings from this man, and perhaps even I had personally suffered from him, our hearts still ached to hear his verdict. We knew that he had been forced by the Germans to behave that way. Few people could withstand those tests; why should the gentiles be the ones to judge them?!

After that incident, the girls on our kibbutz were flooded with letters calling us to come and testify about the actions of a kapo or someone else who had behaved improperly. We knew that all the Poles wanted to do was to continue to harass the Jews—and now under the guise of justice, no less! Of course we paid no attention to the letters. We did not think it was right for us to get involved in handing over our brethren to the gentiles.

You Murdered and Inherited?

Weddings began to take place in our kibbutz. The girls established new homes one after another; Jews from Krakow married girls from Tarnow, and vice versa. Various *shidduchim* were made between the two centers, and there were also those who came from the kibbutzim in Lodz, Chenstochow, and Sosnovtza.

A small Jewish community began to take root. Here and there, one could find *minyanim* gathered in a house provided by the Jewish community.

But the ground still burned beneath our feet!

We still encountered displays of anti-Semitism. I saw a young Pole holding a silver goblet that he apparently stole from a Jewish home, and calling to his friends, "Look at this goblet! The Jews slaughtered our son and filled the goblet with blood and then drank it!"

And everyone screamed back heatedly, "Come, let's all go kill the Jews!"

I heard that there were poor Jews in the house nearby and the gentiles assaulted them. They called the police, who came...and helped the hooligans beat the Jews.

A woman who worked at the police station told me that she met a Jew and told him about what was happening. He went with more police officers and they halted the pogrom.

The anti-Semitic incidents continued: In the summer of 5705/1945, a woman was killed in Krakow; a year later, in 1946, a terrible pogrom took place in Kielce, Poland. Forty-two Yidden who had survived the war met their deaths in the pogrom. They had been living in Kielce and wanted to rehabilitate their lives, but were murdered by lowly gentiles.

Everyone felt the hatred simmering in Poland wherever they went. The non-Jews would sneer, "Hey, you came back? They didn't kill you all?!"

Every so often we received anonymous letters with threats, such as, "We'll slaughter and kill you all."

Once, a group of us girls stood at the train station in Krakow and the Poles noticed us. They shamelessly called to us: "So many Jews are left alive?! Too bad the Germans didn't kill you all!"

Woe unto he who returned to the home where he had lived before the war. Woe to him if he noticed in his home or at the neighbors' a tablecloth or other household goods that had once belonged to him. It was forbidden to say a word! Anyone who made a remark was risking his life.

Jews who had hidden valuables before the war, in the courtyards of their homes or in the nearby forest, returned after the war to the hiding places to search for their treasures. For extra safety, they took a police officer with them. But it often happened that the officer himself killed the Jew and took the valuables. That's why most people relinquished their assets—they were too frightened to return to the hiding places to retrieve them.

⌐⊗⌐

The prominent *rabbanim* who lived on the men's kibbutz guided us in our new lives. The sight of *rabbanim* gave the non-Jews no peace, and we feared that one day, they would attack us.

In light of all this, and after the pogroms, we decided that while it was very congenial for us on the kibbutz—some of us had even married and established homes—we had to flee from that bloody land.

First we moved to the large kibbutz in Lodz; we felt safer there. Families who had spent the war years in Russia gathered in Lodz, and we, the individual survivors, one or two from a family, joined them.

21

THE CHILDREN FROM THE CONVENT

T he Nazi Satan waged a mighty battle against…the Jewish child.

One million children were annihilated during the Holocaust, in all kinds of cruel and bestial ways. The tzaddik, HaRav Mendele of Pabianicz, *zt"l*, explained this phenomenon after witnessing a Nazi soldier trample a little baby. "How do we know that the sun is shining? When it is so strong we cannot look at it. How do we know that a Jewish child glows and illuminates? Because the Satan cannot stand its brilliance…"

I hadn't seen a Jewish child in a very long time. In my eyes, a child symbolized goodness and purity, which had been eradicated under the boots of evil and cruelty.

It's easy to imagine how excited I was when I heard that a baby had been born in the refugee kibbutz, and that a bris was being planned for him!

It was a very significant event that excited all of the survivors. Again, the declaration was emerging: the eternity of Am Yisrael is guaranteed! Again, the blood covenant between Am Yisrael and *HaKadosh Baruch Hu* was being forged, and the words, "*Bedamayich chayi*, by your blood you shall live," infused life into our dry bones.

I was sent with my friends to buy some medicine for the baby. I went with lighthearted steps, feeling a special sense of mission as I purchased something that a pure Jewish baby needed.

The new babies that were born were children of families who had returned from Russia to Poland. The refugees from Poland married one after another, and after a year, once again, babies were born and the sounds of their laughter and crying filled the air, heralding hope for the future.

Nevertheless, we knew we were living here on borrowed time. Poland was under Russian control, and there was the constant danger that borders would suddenly close on us and we would not be able to get out. Indeed, after a short time, leaving Poland became exceedingly difficult.

Even before the gates closed, the heads of the Vaad Hatzolah of *rabbanim* from America and Eretz Yisrael urged the survivors to leave Poland before it was too late.

At that time, I heard about Rebbetzin Recha Sternbuch of Switzerland; she was the daughter of HaRav Rottenberg, *Hy"d*, the rav of the Machzikei Hadas community in Antwerp, Belgium. She was a righteous woman who devoted herself to saving Jews during the war. She continued her efforts after the war was over, and came to Poland to extract survivors from that bloody land. Even in Lodz, where the Jews were more organized and had already established a yeshivah—she urged them to leave Poland. *Leave, leave, get out*…that was the message.

After the pogroms, everyone took these warnings seriously and began to think in practical terms about leaving Poland.

Nightmares

The big kibbutz in Lodz was suddenly teeming with little children, orphaned refugees who had been rescued in secret operations and brought to us.

Again, I saw children wherever I went. No, they were actually little adults! Some of them had experienced things that even adults would have a hard time dealing with.

There were little girls who had been concealed in gentile homes for years. Other children were rescued from convents. The Hatzolah activists put their lives in peril and abducted the children from their hiding places. Alternatively, they paid a very high ransom to redeem them.

I will never forget the fear in the eyes of two girls who came to us from the convent in Krakow. The older of the two was about nine. They were very close to one another and knew they were Jews. Having suffered abuse and hunger in the convent, they wanted to escape.

One day, the girls heard a rumor that the war was over and that the Jews were beginning to return to Krakow. They sought a way to escape from the convent.

When the girls managed to slip out one day, they walked in the streets asking people, "Where is the Jewish community?"

People who they met brought them to our refugee kibbutz, informing us they were Jewish girls who had run away from a Polish convent.

Despite the fact that they came of their own free will, they looked terrified. The first night, they buried their heads under their pillows and cried bitterly.

I placed a gentle hand on their hair and asked softly, "Girls, why are you crying?"

My friends also tried to get them to talk, until finally, they blurted out, "We're so afra-a-aid…"

"Afraid?! What are you afraid of, girls?" we asked in surprise.

"When we were in the convent, the mothers (nuns) told us, 'Look girls, how G-d doesn't like the Jews. If He would love you He wouldn't have sent you such terrible troubles, and such an enemy as Hitler. That's proof, girls, that G-d doesn't love the Jews.'"

"And now," the girls cried, "we're so scared because now we're only among Jews, who G-d really doesn't like…"

The girls were prime examples of the spiritual tragedy that had befallen the pure Polish children, in addition to the incomprehensible physical destruction. It took them time to understand that they were fortunate to have found their way back to the Jews.

One day, the aunt of these girls came to our kibbutz. She had heard that they were in the convent and searched for them, until she finally reached us. She took them under her care.

Krisha came to us after having "graduated" from the horrors of Auschwitz. She was a twin. She had a brother, but didn't know what the Germans had done to him. Krisha seemed to have been saved when the Russians reached Auschwitz and the Germans ran away. The children had remained there all alone. The Christians took the children under their auspices, and the noble *askanim* redeemed them for money.

Information about Gila reached the *askanim*, and they abducted her from inside the convent.

Gila was a baby when her parents entrusted her to the nuns. She didn't know the Jewish name her parents had given her, and knew nothing about her past. She was simply without an identity and no one could tell her anything about her parents.

Gila went to Eretz Yisrael. She was placed in Mizrachi institutions and that was the way she was brought up. With time, she became a world famous personality, and earned a fortune, but she had certain principles that she always kept to— perhaps in the merit of the time that she had spent with us on the kibbutz, and certainly in the merit of her parents. Over the years, I maintained contact with her; she gave a lot of *tzedakah* to institutions that did holy work.

My dear friend Gila had three daughters who became *chareidi* and established beautiful families.

Mrs. Sternbuch and her group worked effectively and devoted themselves to the children who had been rescued by the the Vaad Hatzolah. Regretfully, despite the intense work, many children remained in gentile hands, their souls and the souls of their children still held captive until the arrival of the Redemption, when Hashem will gather all of them from east and west, north and south, together again.

I Become A Counselor

One day, Mrs. Sternbuch announced, "We have made arrangements for a large transport of children to leave Poland, and you, ten girls from the kibbutz, will be their counselors!"

The children did not have official paperwork proving their Judaism, and the convents were demanding to get them back, by force of the law. That's why the *askanim* worked rapidly to get them out of Poland, preparing legal Polish passports for them. The transport was comprised of five hundred people, most of them children.

All those in the transport were classified as "children." There were also adult "children" two years older than us, and we, in our capacity "supervised" them. There were also adults who sneaked onto the transport.

They took us to the city of Beckum, where there was an orphanage run by R' Marmorstein, a Gerrer *chassid*. Among the workers there was Mrs. Lederman, who later moved to Paris.

More children joined us in Beckum. Some of them came with one parent, others with none. There were parents who wanted to send their children ahead of them, before the Iron Curtain would fall on Communist Poland.

We were ordered to board the cars of an American train provided by UNRRA (a relief organization for survivors). We traveled with HaRav Wasserman and the UNRRA people to the border.

At the border there was an inspection and all those who had sneaked on without legal passports were not allowed to continue. The poor people had to get off the train while we continued to travel with the children.

Poland remained behind.

I did not wave goodbye. I fled with my friends and the children to the unknown future.

We reached Czechoslovakia, which was then a liberal, non-Communist country. Czechoslovakia treated the refugees benevolently, ultimately becoming the host country for the first Knessiah Gedolah of Agudas Yisrael after the Holocaust.

We stopped three kilometers from Prague, at a place where the Germans had held Jews during the Holocaust. The site lacked even the most basic amenities, but we breathed a sigh of relief! We were out of Communist Poland.

Two doctors came to attend to us, and a handful of Jews who had come about three months earlier managed the kitchen.

As soon as we arrived, we divided the work among ourselves. Each one of the counselors got a group.

"First, we wash the children!" we decided unanimously. They were very neglected and desperate for a good washing and combing.

There were no bathtubs, and we had to ask the kitchen workers to give us hot water.

In order to have enough water, we gathered branches and made a fire outside and put on a huge pot of water. That's how we washed the children and were then able to comb their hair.

Golda

It was relatively late one evening and we were talking amongst ourselves. "Golda's not falling asleep again!" we told each other. Golda was a small, short child, and naturally, we placed her and her cousin in the seven- and eight-year-old group. We insisted on the children going to sleep at eight o'clock, but Golda never fell asleep then. We would point out to her that she wasn't sleeping even though everyone else was.

One day, Golda mustered up the courage to approach us. "I want to talk to you and tell you my secret..." she said.

We listened curiously. "You are always angry that I am not listening and don't fall asleep at eight o'clock like all the children. I have to tell you that *I'm already fourteen years old*, but I never grew like everyone...How can a fourteen-year-old girl fall asleep so early with all the little kids?!"

We listened to her, shocked and pained all at once. We admitted that it hadn't been right to treat her that way, but it wasn't our fault; we didn't know. Of course, we moved Golda to the older group.

Golda established a beautiful family in Yerushalayim; she has three sons who are *talmidei chachamim*, and a daughter who married a ben Torah, as well as many grandchildren. Golda merited to have many miracles performed for her by Hashem (as I will expound on later.)

We were extremely busy with the children in Czechoslovakia.

One of the children contracted an ear infection. The counselor obtained some cotton-tipped sticks for him, but of course, they were useless. On Shabbos, the child's pain intensified, his fever rose and the doctor said we had to go to the hospital. As his counselors, we were obliged to accompany him.

We arrived at the hospital at 9:50; by ten o'clock he was already on the operating table. The infection had spread and had nearly reached his brain. The Czech team at the hospital treated the child and us very courteously.

Days passed as we cared for the children. Every so often we traveled to Prague to see the beautiful city, especially its unique shul.

But if we thought that we'd find rest for our weary feet, we were mistaken. Slowly, the anti-Semitism in Czechoslovakia intensified; there, too, the Communists took over. The Vaad Hatzolah, with the Joint and Agudas Yisrael, came to help us continue our journey to a freer country.

The next destination was France.

We were loaded onto a train again. A few small families also joined us. The new adults who joined were each assigned a job:

one was the *melamed* of the children, another was a kitchen worker and so forth. Everyone was considered part of the staff that cared for the children.

The train traveled on and on, sometimes stopping for long periods of time. After a very long journey, we reached our destination.

With Warmth and Love

We arrived in France on Erev Yom Kippur and settled in a beautiful building with a few floors, with more than 200 rooms. The building had been purchased and prepared for us by the Vaad Hatzolah.

"*Seudas hamafsekes*" was the first thing on our minds. The purifying atmosphere of the impending day permeated the air and our hearts…

We entered a large hall with the children, where a delicious, nutritious meal was waiting for us. It had been prepared by Jewish youths from the Ezra movement.

I continued working tirelessly to care for the children, while preparing them for the Holy Day. I taught them the meaning of the words of the Yom Kippur prayers and other things about the special day. The two directors divided the children into classes. Rav Silberberg and his brother-in-law, Rav Weiss (the husband of my friend Gita), began to teach the children, literally from aleph-bais.

This was no simple feat! These children were ignorant of even basic Jewish concepts; they had been torn away from their parents while they were babies. Remember, in Poland, the war had lasted more than five years!

There were orphans who had spent the war years in Russia and were placed in a Russian orphanage. After the war, they were redeemed, and they came to us without any Jewish knowledge.

Many children did not remember their fathers and mothers… their only memories were of the gentile people from the villages…

We had a very heavy responsibility and a herculean task. We had to take the place of vanished mothers and fathers, and to provide a lot of warmth and boundless love. I hope that we succeeded in giving them all they needed.

I will never forget those little children, whose images remain in my mind's eye to this day…

As time passed, we were flooded with requests from American families wanting to adopt a child.

Some of the children asked to be transferred to relatives in America. Others formed close ties with American couples who came and adopted them.

In the interim, representatives from Eretz Yisrael also visited us and took care of the children.

We often traveled to the *yeshivah gedolah* that had been established in the village of Baie in France. Former yeshivah students, most of them from Lithuania, gathered there, but there were also *chassidishe bochurim*, including some from Yeshivas Chachmei Lublin in Poland. We would listen to rousing *drashos* that gave us *chizuk*. The *rabbanim* tried constantly to infuse us with hope and comfort, and most importantly, to instill a love of Torah and a love of Hashem in our battered hearts.

Every so often, one of the *rabbanim* from the yeshivah honored us with a visit, and spoke to the orphaned children in our Children's House.

22

A NEW LIFE

I bent over a bowl full of eggs together with my friend. "There, thirty-six!" one of the girls cried excitedly, and we began to beat the eggs for the *lekach* cake for our friend's wedding.

The only wedding dress we had was washed and passed around to all the *kallahs*. The seamstresses among us expanded it or took it in as necessary, lengthening and shortening. We baked rolls for the wedding meal. One woman regularly cooked the fish, and Reb Yom Tov Ehrlich came to enhance the *simchah* with his songs and rhymes. The French government also gave a grant and financial aid to couples who married.

The children from the Children's House slowly found their places, one by one. My friends and I moved to Aix-les-Bains, near Paris, and the Joint took us under its auspices.

Many survivors got married in Paris to fellow survivors, mostly those who had learned in Lithuanian yeshivos before the war. *Chassidim* of Ger, Bobov, Belz, and Chabad also organized and established homes; they got married in *shteiblach* to perpetuate their holy legacies.

The weddings were simple, no-frills affairs, and there was a lot of genuine Jewish joy. At the same time, the hearts of the *chassan* and *kallah* longed for their parents and siblings, who participated in their wedding in spirit only. The bodies had been burned in the furnaces or murdered in other barbaric ways.

The young couples did not receive dowries or support of any kind. Their expectations were minimal. Each couple received a room or half a room adjacent to a kitchen, and they whispered thanks to Hashem for the merit to build a home in Am Yisrael... Who had dreamed of this while in the camps, when we'd been humiliated to the lowest depths and the future seemed so hopeless?! When the pinnacle of our dreams was a piece of bread—who thought we'd ever establish families?!

Time passed quickly. There was a group of girls left who had not yet found their matches. Most of us wanted to go to America, while a small group intended to go to Eretz Yisrael, even though *aliyah* was illegal at that time.

Meanwhile, we lived in a very pretty part of Aix-les-Bains, in a small apartment near the Agudas Yisrael offices. We spent many *Shabbasos* in Baie, near the yeshivah of survivors and refugees.

A Personal Introspection

Personally, I conducted my own introspection...

I had eight dear brothers and sisters. I had been blessed with wonderful parents. Everyone had been taken, and I was the only one to survive.

Why???

Divine *Hashgachah* had chosen me to remain the only one from my beautiful family. I wasn't the smartest or the best of them. Why had I been chosen to survive?! Why had I been decreed to live?!

The ways of Hashem are concealed. What do we understand about Heavenly considerations? *HaKadosh Baruch Hu* on High was the One to decide that I would be the lone survivor.

But it would not be for naught. I was keenly aware of the *Hashgachah pratis* that had guided my every step in the most difficult, dangerous moments. How many times had I faced death—and then survived?!

Mah ashiv l'Hashem?! I thought about this constantly during the day, and pondered it at night as I tried to sleep. I had to do something with my life! I had to find a special significance to the precious life Hashem granted me. The gift of life was not to be taken for granted. I had to fulfill my mission, my destiny...

My thoughts took me in the direction of *ahavas Torah* and appreciation for Torah.

I had absorbed the concept of honoring the holy Torah with every fiber of my being, in my far-off home that had long since disappeared. Torah was the joy of my parents' hearts, *Hy"d*.

I remembered my elderly grandfather, my memories of him floating through my mind. He was a genuine *talmid chacham*; he was always either learning from a *sefer*, reciting Tehillim or otherwise involved in Torah. I was a little girl when his image was etched into my soul, and it was this image that stood in my mind at this crucial crossroads in my life, and clarifying for me exactly my purpose in life: a life of Torah.

I had heard that my grandfather and another Jew were the first to open the old *bais medrash* every day at four in the morning. Before he departed this world, he had a wondrous vision of a *minyan* of men wrapped in *talleisim,* standing around his bed. These were sublime experiences, similar to those that great *tzaddikim* saw before their passing.

Perhaps it was his great merit that had helped me survive.

I felt that I needed to build a true life of Torah, a life that would express my tremendous gratitude to *HaKadosh Baruch Hu* for accompanying me through the travails of the Holocaust and keeping me alive.

I wanted to dedicate my life to helping a ben Torah, one who would devote his days and nights only to the holy Torah.

Ach, a life of Torah, the most wonderful thing a Yid could strive for! A woman cannot, and is not commanded to, learn, but if I would marry a tremendous *talmid chacham* and a lofty personality, I could serve him and be a helpmate to him—and in this way I would merit to give praise to Hashem in a tangible, active way, all the time.[1]

Just One Year

One of the survivors in the large yeshivah in the town of Baie was the renowned genius HaRav Mordechai Pogromansky, *zt"l*. He was a *talmid chacham* and tzaddik, whom *gedolei Yisrael* respected and held in great esteem.

I would listen to the *drashos* he delivered to the survivors, and I had an idea—this was the *talmid chacham* I was looking for, even though there was a great difference in our ages.

My friend, Rebbetzin Shaindel Miller, who was with me in Aix-les-Bains, conveyed my sentiments to her husband, HaRav Meir Miller, *zt"l*, who was close to Reb Mordechai.

A short time later, we became engaged, and I was overjoyed. I felt

---

1. Her son, the Sassov-Monsey Rebbe, *shlita* says:

   Such lofty aspirations at the end of a physical, spiritual, and emotional Holocaust were seldom found. Every girl who survived wanted to shake off the ashes of the destruction, marry and begin a new life. There were hardly any girls who refrained from marrying because they were seeking an exceptional *talmid chacham*, a rarity to find.

   My mother, *a"h*, who decided to devote her life to Torah, succeeded in realizing her aspirations. In her greatness, she didn't even think of being proud of the fact that she married one of the most admired *gedolei hador*. To her it seemed simple and self-understood, because that was her job in life!

a tremendous sense of satisfaction at fulfilling my objective. My life became significant, I merited to bring *nachas* to the Creator. I was kept alive to serve a great person, a *talmid chacham* and *oved Hashem*!

Our wedding was held on Rosh Chodesh Adar 5709/1949, and was attended by the *rabbanim* who were then in Paris. It was a large, special wedding, as was fitting for such an eminent person.

That night, Reb Shalom Tzvi HaKohen Shapiro, one of the *gaonim* of the generation, also got married. Mrs. Recha Sternbuch prepared me and my friend, Rebbetzin Shapiro, for our weddings.

After the wedding, we moved to Versailles, to be near the yeshivah in Baie. Reb Mordechai remained connected to the students of the yeshivah and many continued to seek his advice and guidance.

I will never forget the visit of of Rav Yosef Shlomo Kahaneman of Ponovezh, who came from Eretz Yisrael. He spoke at length with Reb Mordechai and invited him to serve as *rosh yeshivah* of Ponovezh in Bnei Brak. Reb Mordechai was hesitant to accept the request, fearing that by taking the job he would cause others to get upset.

In any case, it soon became irrelevant…

In actuality, Reb Mordechai had fallen ill before the wedding but the doctors were unable to diagnose the illness. Three months after we got married, his illness worsened, and the Sternbuch family invited us to Switzerland, where Reb Mordechai could be treated.

We moved to Switzerland, *davening* to Hashem that salvation lay there. We went from one hospital to another, and all the doctors took his illness very seriously.

Many good Jews made sure I had no financial worries or technical arrangements to be busy with. Reb Wolf Rosengarten and Rebbetzin Sternbuch would send clothes and other things that I needed to the hospital through Rebbetzin Shapiro.

At the hospital I acquired a dear friend, Rebbetzin Rachel Sarna, the wife of HaRav Chaim Sarna, Rosh Yeshivas Chevron, and the daughter-in-law of HaRav Yechezkel Sarna. She, too, had come for medical treatment. The friendship lasted for the rest of our lives; we lived like two sisters and she ultimately became a very caring aunt to my children.

Reb Mordechai accepted his illness with love and astounded those around him with his noble comportment. Once, before a surgical procedure, he asked not to be sedated! If he was destined to suffer, he wanted to feel the suffering and accept it! The doctors were astonished at his tremendous spirit.

I was at the Sternbuch home when I received the tragic news that Reb Mordechai, my pious husband, had passed away...

He was just 46 years old.

Again I was alone...The decree had been rendered; this is what Divine *Hashgachah* wanted. I accompanied him on his final journey on this earth on the day of our first anniversary.

Gedolei hador said that Reb Mordechai had been worthy of effecting a spiritual *mussar* revolution, like Reb Yisrael Salanter in his time, but the generation did not merit it...

Reb Mordechai was buried in Zichron Meir in Bnei Brak, with the Torah world, headed by the Chazon Ish, tearfully accompanying him. Those who were there testified that it was one of the few times that the Chazon Ish was witnessed crying.

I remained alone in the world, but Hashem did not abandon me. I was surrounded by wonderful, caring people.

I lived at the Sternbuchs for another year and they hosted me warmly. I would bake challos and rolls for sick survivors who lay in isolation in a gentile environment. In our times, most patients receive antibiotics, but then, in order to heal, people had to spend years living in isolation in a sanatorium.

The condition of these patients was heart wrenching. We

couldn't send them wine for Kiddush, only small rolls. It was a tremendous mitzvah to visit these sick people, whose litany of suffering had yet to come to an end.

HaRav Mordechai Pogromansky, zt"l, was one of the gaonim *of Yeshivas Telz, a* talmid chacham *and expert in both* nigleh *and* nistar, *as well as being humble and constantly fleeing honor and rabbinical positions.* Gedolei Yisrael *were in awe of him and spoke wondrously of him.*

In the book "Yovel Hameah L'Yeshivas Telz," the Rosh Yeshivah HaRav Mordechai Gifter brings remarkable stories about Reb Mordechai Pogromansky. He used to review fifty pages of Gemara a day. He was an expert in all parts of Torah, as well as being a tzaddik and chassid *in his mitzvah observance and in his behavior. He was a* baal mussar *and* mashpia *for those near and far.*

Reb Mordechai survived the war, and was one of the pillars of fire that led the camp after the war. One prominent refugee camp was centered around the yeshivah in Baie near Paris, where talmidim *of the yeshivos in Lita and Poland and other places came together. Reb Mordechai was the coordinating and leading figure, and everyone respected him and looked up to him as a role model. Many thought of him as their "urim ve'teumim," and an address for all their problems. The refugees who were with him testified that even after the war, he was still proficient in the most complex* sugyos *in Shas, as though he had learned them the day before.*

Zecher tzaddik livrachah.

23

THE ANSWER TO ALL THE QUESTIONS

My greatest wish was to travel to Eretz Yisrael; I longed for the moment I would be able to leave Europe, which I associated with so much loss.

My dream was realized shortly afterward.

Eretz Yisrael welcomed me with open arms. Rabbi and Rebbetzin Miller—my acquaintances from Aix-les-Bains— brought me into their home warmly and gave me a wonderful feeling of being wanted.

It was an exceptional gesture on their part!

My friendship with Rebbetzin Miller lasted for the rest of our lives. In time, she became a beloved "aunt" to my children.

Once I was in Eretz Yisrael, I was cared for by wonderful Yidden, acquaintances of myself and Reb Mordechai. With sensitivity and understanding, they all tried to help me and provide whatever I needed. My good friends from the kibbutzim in Tarnow and Lodz remained in close contact.

Five and a half years passed, and once again, I was granted a great *zechus* when I married the Sassover Rebbe. I had the privilege of establishing a beautiful family, *bechasdei Hashem*.

The *tefillah* that I always carried in my heart was that my children should follow the path of their forebears, and grow up in a way that befit our holy ancestors.

The Rebbe had a great vision: he aspired to establish a real chassidic yeshivah. Thus he established Kiryas Yismach Moshe in Eretz Yisrael, where the sounds of Torah and Chassidus resonate, bringing his wondrous dream to fruition.

While in the midst of this undertaking, the Rebbe fell ill and became bedridden…

By the time our apartment in Yismach Moshe was ready, the Rebbe was already very sick. Before we moved in he had one request: "Please, buy me a Shas! I can't move into a house that doesn't have a Shas."

Those were his aspirations and desires, even in the midst of his painful suffering.

Before we purchased anything else for the apartment—a refrigerator, oven, or table—we purchased the Shas. It was the crowning glory of our home.

The most burning of all my questions, which accompanied me by day and tortured me at night, was why I had remained alive. "Everyone else went up On High like a pure sacrifice, and I was chosen to survive. Why?!" It was a question I would often ask the Rebbe.

"You must understand," he explained to me, and I never tired of hearing his answer, "we see clearly that it was destined from

Above that you specifically should become a mother, and raise Yosef Dovid, Henoch, Moishe'le, Shloime'le, and Esther..."

His words were like a balm on my aching heart, because that is the eternal answer.

It is the *ruach hakdoesh* that calls to all the survivors of the camps, raises them from the ashes and the depths of suffering, with a comforting call: "*Kein yirbeh,* so should he multiply!"

May these words be a memory for those who perished *al kiddush Hashem*, and may their souls be ensconced in eternal life.

CHAPTERS OF SONG

IN TRIBUTE TO AN EXCEPTIONAL MOTHER

By:

Her son, the Sassov-Monsey Rebbe, *shlita*
Her daughter, Rebbetzin Esther Rabinowitz, *shetichyeh*

This is just a glimpse into the lofty personality that was our mother—because nothing we could write would be enough.

Her life full of challenges became her banner, elevating her and connecting her to her Creator.

WHAT DOES HASHEM ASK OF ME

The Sassov-Monsey Rebbe's story begins where the Rebbetzin's moving story, that she shared from the depths of her soul, ends. With the deepest admiration, he shares the continuation of the tumultuous life of his mother, Rebbetzin Bluma Teitelbaum, a"h, which was a lesson in firm faith in the face of the challenges that awaited her at every turn.

This chapter also includes the life story and memories of his father, the Sassover Rebbe, zt"l.

The Holocaust did not only destroy bodies, it also seared souls. Many Yidden left their roots and tossed away their faith after having been through Gehinnom in this world. They had questions and doubts, but we know that the ways of Hashem are hidden from us.

By contrast, there were Yidden whose faith intensified *because of the Holocaust*. The thought that constantly guided them and helped them shake off the ashes was, "Divine Providence left me alive—which means that He expects something of me; I have been entrusted with a great responsibility."

That was the axis upon which my mother's trouble-filled life revolved. She always sensed that her role in this world was to discover what Hashem was asking of her, and to justify the responsibility that had been placed upon her from Above, by Hashem Who had allowed her to survive the Holocaust.

The pure Bais Yaakov *chinuch* was deeply ingrained in my mother's psyche. Her love of Torah intensified even after the war, and she sensed that her mission in this world was to establish her home with a *talmid chacham*. After the liberation, she traveled to Paris as a children's counselor. Most of her friends married quickly and built homes, but she wasn't satisfied with the suggestions she was receiving.

She was looking for an outstanding *talmid chacham*...

It was a rare and virtually unrealistic request. Mother was an orphan from both parents, had nothing to her name, and was alone after all her suffering—yet, she did not allow reality to confuse her. She pleaded and *davened* to Hashem—and ultimately, she found what she was looking for in 5709/1949, when she married HaRav Mordechai Pogromansky, *zt"l*.

Reb Mordechai was a *talmid chacham* and tzaddik, truly an elevated person. When he met my mother, he told her the truth about his precarious health, and he made it clear that he was not sure how long he would live "If he survived the horrors of the war, he can also overcome the illness," some people claimed.

My mother was deeply impressed by his forthrightness and honesty, in addition to all his other attributes. She agreed to the *shidduch* and they had a large wedding for those times.

Three months after the wedding, Reb Mordechai fell ill and was hospitalized in Paris. Due to the war, medical services in

France were limited, which is why they were sent to Switzerland. At the famed Sternbuch home, they experienced exceptional *hachnassas orchim*, and for several months, Reb Mordechai was in and out of hospitals.

Only a few months later, Reb Mordechai passed away. His *levayah* took place on their first anniversary.

It's hard to fathom the depths of my mother's pain in the face of this tragedy. She had no relatives, no one to turn to… Most of her friends were married, some already had children who filled their homes with joy and hope. She had married late, after insisting on waiting for a Torah scholar, and then, after seeing her wishes fulfilled, he passed away…

An average person would have probably given up in despair after such a tragedy. But not Mother—absolutely not!

She was driven by tremendous fortitude. She didn't raise her hands in despair, because she was following her holy mission in life: doing the Will of Hashem.

The *Chalitzah*

Reb Mordechai passed away without leaving any children, and therefore, Mother was obligated to perform *chalitzah*.

As a youth, Reb Mordechai had traveled to study at the yeshivos of Lithuania, and hardly ever visited home. One day, he received a letter telling him that he had become a big brother to a baby boy. His mother had passed away some time before, and his father had married another woman. After a few years, a short time after his father also passed away—the brother was born, and named for his father, Eliyahu.

Reb Mordechai hardly knew his younger brother. After the war he went to great efforts to locate him and find out more about him, and was pleased to learn that he had survived, and was living in the United States. They remained in contact by writing letters.

When Reb Mordechai realized that his illness was terminal, he realized that his wife, our mother, would have to receive *chalitzah* from his brother, and thus made the arrangements with his brother before his *petirah*. This was in 5710/1950, before the age of direct flights. The brother was not religious and Reb Mordechai asked before his passing that the *chalitzah* should be carried out without causing *chillul Shabbos* or eating *treif* food. When it became relevant, the Ponovezher Rav got involved, and received specific guidance from the Chazon Ish. The Chazon Ish, with his *ruach hakodesh*, instructed them how to act and how to help Mother so it would be performed properly.

The *chalitzah* took place in Switzerland.

After that, my mother went to Eretz Yisrael, and her goal in life continued to guide her. She still aspired to be the wife of a *talmid chacham*...a tzaddik...

HaRav Meir Miller, a prominent Torah scholar, was very close to Reb Mordechai in Baie, France. His wife had been with my mother in Aix-les-Bains. Now they opened their home to Mother, the widow of Reb Mordechai. For five years, their home in Bat Yam was my mother's home, where she lived with dignity until her second marriage in 5715/1955.

Mother went to work each day at the Goldfinger diamond factory in Tel Aviv. She tried not to live off other's people's *chessed*, and helped care for the little children in the Miller home. To this day, they remember her for this, and the families remain close.

Every so often, Mother would go to the Chazon Ish to mention her name for a *yeshuah*. She didn't desist from her aspirations of being the wife of a *talmid chacham*. Despite the passing time, she didn't give up. She had been through so much in her life: she was 17 when the war broke out, and endured six years of horrors, until the age of 23. When she was 27, she married for the first time, and was widowed a year later. Five more years of widowhood passed until her time finally came; she found her match, my father, the Sassover Rebbe, *zt"l*.

The Sassover Rebbe, *zt"l*

My father, HaRav Chananya Yom Tov Lipa, the Sassover Rebbe *zt"l*, was a true tzaddik, a tremendous *talmid chacham* and *oved Hashem* who had exceptionally refined *middos*. Throughout the various stops in his life, he was very active in disseminating Torah and in establishing legions of *talmidim* who would serve Hashem.

My father was born in 5665/1905 to his father, HaRav Chanoch Henoch of Sassov, *zt"l*, the son of the Rebbe, R' Yosef Dovid of Sassov, *zt"l*, the son of HaRav Shlomo of Sassov, *zt"l*, the son of HaRav Chanoch Henoch of Alesk, *zt"l*, who was the son-in-law of the Sar Shalom of Belz, *zt"l*.

In 5684/1924 my father married his cousin, Rebbetzin Chaya Roisa, *a"h*, the daughter of the Satmar Rebbe, HaRav Yoel Teitelbaum *zt"l* (who was my father's uncle). From that point on, he was his father-in-law's right-hand man in prominent communities, where he served as *rosh yeshivah* first in Orshiva, and then in Krali. Around 5692/1932, the Rebbe and his father-in-law, *zt"l*, began to serve in the city of Satmar.

My father inculcated the *talmidim* of the yeshivah with the right path, and delivered *shiurim* that were forever etched on the hearts of his students. Many Satmar *chassidim* numbered among his students, and his image accompanied them throughout their lives. Later, my father became the rav and head of the Bais Din in Semiheli, and he would return home to Satmar for Shabbos.

My father's brilliance was renowned. He once spoke of an interesting and complicated case that had been presented to him. With his wisdom, he realized that the litigants were deceiving him, and he was spared making a big mistake when he delivered the ruling in Bais Din.

During the Holocaust, my father worked tirelessly to save people and to help refugees get from Poland to Hungary.

Between 1939 and 1944, Hungary was relatively calm, while in most of Europe the war machine was working full force. Hungary was already a partner in the Reich and the Jews were drafted to the army, but the deportations of the Jews had not yet begun in Hungary.

Many Jews fled from Poland to Hungary at great risk; anyone who was caught was sent back to his country of origin. Once the refugees did succeed in getting into Hungary, my father helped them find hiding places and provided for their needs.

My grandfather, the Rebbe Rav Henoch, *zt"l*, my father's father, lived in Sassov, located near Lemberg in Galicia, until World War I. Sassov was very close to the border with Russia, and therefore, the family fled from there. They endured many tribulations, including hunger, and moved to Lemberg. They never returned to Sassov, which was completely destroyed.

My grandfather became the rav of the city of Kratzky in Czechoslovakia. In 1939, Hitler captured Czechoslovakia and gave part of it to Hungary.

My grandfather was now in great danger. He was a Polish

citizen and the Hungarians repatriated all Polish citizens. My grandfather and his family picked up again and moved to Satmar, a large city where it was easy to hide. They lived in my father's house between 1940 and 1943, and my grandfather conducted his court from there. My grandfather, the Rebbe, passed away in Satmar during the war, on 7 Cheshvan 1942, and was laid to rest in Satmar.

Hungary was captured on 24 Adar 5704 in a lightening quick operation, and the conquerors were eager for blood. Just a few weeks later, the Germans began the transports of the Jews to the camps in Poland.

Run!!! my father decided. Those were the initial weeks of the occupation, before the ghettos were hermetically sealed. Escape was still possible, and my father, his wife, and his sister, who was seven and a half years old at the time, (later Rebbetzin Mattel Zaks, *tlita*, of the United States, the widow of Rav Gershon Zaks, *zt"l*, a grandson of the Chafetz Chaim, *zt"l*) fled by train from Satmar to Klausenberg, disguised as non-Jews.

In Klausenberg lived a Satmar *chassid* named Reb Yirmiyahu Tessler, and the escapees arrived at his house. Reb Yirmiyah knew border smugglers and directed them to the right one. With the help of the smugglers, the three arrived in Temeshvar, Romania.

The city of Temeshvar was relatively safe, but the authorities were constantly searching for refugees who had infiltrated. My father continued his flight to Bucharest, and when he sensed danger there, he decided to board a ship to Eretz Yisrael.

It was 1944. Three ships set out at the same time for Eretz Yisrael. Two of them were sunk by the British just before they reached their destination, and only the ship that my father was on arrived intact.

My father, his wife, and his sister were sent to Cyprus, from which they were transferred to Atlit; ultimately they reached Yerushalayim.

The Satmar shul located on Yoel Street in Yerushalayim was built in 5693/1933 by the *chassidim* after the Satmar Rebbe, HaRav Yoel, visited Eretz Yisrael.

When my father arrived, he was appointed the rav of the Satmar community in Yerushalayim. Together with the *chassidim*, he established Yeshivas Yitav Lev and was appointed the *rosh yeshivah.* After the Holocaust, at the end of 5705/1945, the Satmar Rebbe came to Eretz Yisrael and lived there for about a year, after which he moved to America. My father remained in Yerushalayim and continued to run the yeshivah and *bais medrash.*

In 1948, Eretz Yisrael was in a stormy state. The War of Independence and the many events it engendered drew the residents into a whirlpool of danger and worry. The Satmar Rebbe sent his son-in-law, my father, and his daughter, Rebbetzin Chaya Roisa, a telegram, asking them to come to America to escape the perils of the war.

Again my father picked up his wandering stick, this time heading to America. He moved with the Rebbetzin and his sister to America and settled in Manhattan, where he established the Sassover Bais Medrash. He lived there until 1954, when his Rebbetzin, Chaya Roisa, passed away.

They had been married for thirty years; they did not have children.

My father remained alone and he traveled back to Eretz Yisrael to imbibe the air there and to seek comfort...

Brief Years of Resurrection and Vision

My father was fifty years old at the time, and wanted to marry someone who could still have children. When Mother—the young widow of Rav Mordechai Pogromansky—was suggested for him, he agreed.

After their meeting, Mother happily informed the matchmaker that she was impressed by his Torah knowledge and regal bearing, as he wore the rabbinic garb of a Rebbe. She felt that her greatest wishes had been answered.

There was one small concern that Mother had, and she shared what was on her mind with a friend: "He might ask me to cover my *sheitel*, and I am not used to that…"

"He didn't ask, so don't worry," her friend soothed her.

They wedding took place in Elul 5715/1955, and it didn't take long for my father to ask her to cover her *sheitel*.

She willingly acquiesced to his request. With time he encouraged her to expand the head covering, and she agreed wholeheartedly. In time, she told us, "Dear children, I was so inspired by your father that all I wanted was that he should be pleased…I thought to myself: If I merited such a prominent husband, and he asks something of me, how can I refuse?!"

My father also deeply respected his wife for her piety and her talents. Mother was very learned; she had a brilliant mind and loved to learn. Among other things, she studied Mishnayos and Chumash with Rashi. Her entire family, who had perished, had been very talented.

Mother also excelled in her knowledge of foreign languages and wrote beautifully. Wherever she went in her life, she was able to pick up the language. She spoke six languages: *Lashon Kodesh*, Yiddish, Polish, German, English, and French. In addition, she knew a bit of Russian and Italian.

My father took care of her and deeply respected her. They

lived in a three-story home in Manhattan, and Mother would go up and down from floor to floor many times each day. My father felt bad for the exertion this entailed, and would urge her not to hurry or strain herself too much.

Follow Me In the Desert

Mother really preferred to remain in Eretz Yisrael after her marriage. She had suffered enough, and she wanted to live a peaceful life in the Land of Hashem.

But my father's *bais medrash* was in Manhattan and he asked her to come live in America, reassuring her: "It will only be temporary. I promise you we will come back. I also want to return to the Holy Land, because the purpose of Yidden is in Eretz Yisrael. But in the meantime, that is where my *bais medrash* is, and as soon as we are able, we will come back."

A year after their marriage, my mother gave birth to her oldest son, my brother, the Sassov-Kiryas Yismach Moshe Rebbe of Eretz Yisrael. After his birth, my father promised that they would have his *upsherin* in Meron.

Meanwhile, Hashem bestowed much *chessed* on them, and by the time my brother turned three, two more brothers had been born, and traveling to Eretz Yisrael with three toddlers was too difficult. But my father had promised, and therefore, he calculated the amount it would have cost to travel and sent the money to the poor of Eretz Yisrael.

My parents never abandoned their dream of going back to Eretz Yisrael. In 5718/1958, three years after their marriage, my father began to make frequent trips to Eretz Yisrael. He searched for land upon which he could settle. He surveyed many areas, and finally, in 5722/1962, found land near Bnei Brak upon which he established Kiryas Yismach Moshe.

The first residents moved in at the beginning of 5725/1964, even before the roads were paved. There was no organized transportation or communications yet either.

The five children were born one after another, and in the meantime, my father would travel frequently to Eretz Yisrael to realize his dream, Kiryas Yismach Moshe. Mother remained alone with the children and enabled him to devote himself to his life's work. She did it with a lofty sense of mission.

In the summer of 5724/1964, my father was in Eretz Yisrael, while we remained in America with our devoted mother who took very good care of us. She was helped by a babysitter, a Bais Yaakov student.

Things were going smoothly, until that terrible day...

In Elul 5724/1964, my father held a press conference in Kiryas Yismach Moshe, reporting on the progress of its development and what more needed to be done.

Suddenly, he lost his ability to speak and fell silent.

A few moments of silence passed, and his faculty of speech returned. But it didn't take long for this to happen again. My father hurried to the doctor, who declared, "The problem is in the brain! You have to go to the hospital!"

My father was hospitalized, and the tragic diagnosis was rendered: my father had a growth on his brain and needed to be operated on immediately.

During the operation, Mother was in America, packing up for the urgent trip to Eretz Yisrael to be at her husband's bedside.

We remained alone, five little children, in the capable hands of our babysitter. It was summer vacation and she was able to spend the time caring for us. But after a few weeks, vacation came to an end, and she had to go back to school.

By telephone and through letters, Mother arranged places for us to stay. We moved into the home of my father's brother, the Kirelhauser Rav of Crown Heights. We stayed there from the middle of Elul until after Rosh Hashanah.

During the *Aseres Yemei Teshuvah*, we five little children traveled to Eretz Yisrael.

We arrived after a difficult period and an exhausting flight, and all we wanted was to reunite with our parents, but there was no proper home waiting for us. The apartments in Yismach Moshe were not yet ready. My father was in Hadassah Hospital for treatment, and alternated with convalescence at a hotel in Yerushalayim, while Mother sat at his side and helped care for him.

Feeling that she had to be at his bedside, Mother divided us among families of very giving people: the three "big" boys (the oldest of whom was younger than eight), Yosef Dovid, Henoch, and Moshe, were sent to the home of Rav Yehudah Yoel Miller, *shlita*, in Yerushalayim, a *talmid* of my father from Satmar. While there, I attended the Vizhnitzer Cheder in Yerushalayim.

The two babies, Shlomo'le and Esther, were welcomed into the Stern home in Givat Shaul.

Mother continued to be at my father's bedside in the hospital or at the hotel.

In the winter of 5725/1965, the first building in Kiryas Yismach Moshe was completed. Finally, we had a home!

We children truly rejoiced when we were reunited with our dear parents. My father returned home from the hospital in a wheelchair, with his left side paralyzed, but he was still our beloved father. We were overjoyed to be with our parents once again.

A new and difficult period in our lives began. Each week, my mother accompanied my father for treatment and radiation at Hadassah Hospital in Yerushalayim. Sometimes he was hospitalized for a few days, and she was always there with him.

She hired a *frum* nanny who lived in our house and took care of us.

The treatments did not heal my father, but they did slow down the progression of the disease.

At the beginning of Kislev 5726/1965, his condition deteriorated. My mother was with him in the hospital and we were at home, under the care of our nanny and deeply missing our parents.

My father, the pious tzaddik, passed away on 11 Adar 5726/1966, at the age of 61.

Mother was then 44 years old, and had already suffered so much. She had five young children, the oldest aged nine and the youngest just three and a half.

Mother was engulfed by so many troubles—but they only drew her closer to Hashem. She continued to seek and aspire; what more could she do for her Father in Heaven?! How, in this situation, could she do the most for him?!

My righteous mother retained her noble demeanor. She continued to be the Sassover Rebbetzin in every sense, recognizing the privilege she had been granted: to serve her eminent husband, the Rebbe, for ten and a half years, and to raise their children. She knew that her Divine mission was to be *mechanech* her children, with their prestigious lineage, in the path that would honor their father; to raise the precious treasures in a way that would not shame their forebears.

Indeed, she constantly reminded us that we were children of holy people. She expected us to behave in a way that befitted our status, and told us a lot about our ancestors. She would send us to chassidic courts so that we should absorb our heritage and grow up in the way that our father hoped for.

She devoted her days and nights to her holy mission of raising the children, and later, to finding them good *shidduchim*. Indeed, she was *zocheh* to have her children marry into eminent chassidic courts and the families of famed *tzaddikim*.

In 5732/1972, Mother established a *kollel* in Kiryas Yismach Moshe, and each year, she traveled to America to raise money for it. She managed the *kollel* for many years, guided by the central question that filled her life: what more can I do for Hashem, Who granted me life?

After my marriage, I moved to America, where my father-in-law, *shlita*, lives, and when Mother came for her annual appeal for the *kollel*, she would stay with me.

V'Emunascha Baleilos

In 1979, we discovered that Mother was ill…

It is hard to describe our concern and distress, but Mother was strong and brave; her spirit did not break. For nearly two years, she remained in America for treatment, returning to Eretz Yisrael only for *Yamim Tovim*. During those two years, she did not focus on her illness, but rather worked to strengthen the *kollel* and to increase its income.

Baruch Hashem, she recovered. We spent several good years under the wing of a devoted, pious mother, but at the end of 1990, once again, the illness was detected, this time in her eye. The doctors told us that it would be necessary to remove it and insert a glass eye.

The operation took place at a hospital in Philadelphia. In order to make our stay there more pleasant, a friend brought us cassette tapes from a Holocaust survivor speaking about her past. Mother listened to the story during the long drives and while she was hospitalized.

Then I suggested that we do the same thing, and indeed, she related the riveting and inspiring story that makes up this book.

Mother used her convalescence for other purposes, primarily, strengthening the *kollel* she had established. She also worked on behalf of the large *gemach* she managed, through which she lent large sums of money to the needy.

Throughout that time my righteous wife, Rebbetzin Chana Mindel, *a"h*, the daughter of HaRav Eliyahu Yehoshua Geldzahler, *shlita*, was there for her to provide support and care. Mother spent about four weeks in our home recovering, during which time my rebbetzin catered to her every need. She would clean the incision site and do everything else my mother needed gently and with compassion. She even helped my mother record her life story. May her merits advocate for her in the Upper Worlds. (My rebbetzin passed away after an illness on 26 Sivan 5771/2011; may she be a *melitzas yosher* for our family.)

Baruch Hashem, Mother recovered once again.

A short time passed, and she continued to be active on behalf of Torah and *chessed* causes.

And then again…

In the summer of 5754/1994 Mother didn't feel well. Again we began the rounds of doctors and tests, and during the *Aseres Yemei Teshuvah* of 5755/1994, we were informed that Mother was ill yet a third time. This time, the disease affected her liver.

It was a difficult illness. The doctors wrung their hands in despair; there was little they could do.

The wonderful *ish chessed*, Reb Elimelech Firer, referred us to a hospital in Texas. A strong will to live still coursed within my mother. Despite the fact that the doctors had despaired, she always had the following sentence on her lips: *"M'tor zich nisht meyaesh zein.* We must not despair!"

Mother flew to America. She spent the winter of 5755/1995

in treatment, but it was not effective. All our efforts were for naught.

We marveled at her rock solid *emunas chachamim*, which had characterized her from a very early age. The Skulener Rebbe, *shlita*, sent her to a Spanish healer in Boro Park for massage therapy. There were those who raised an eyebrow at the very idea...What would massages help?

But if the Rebbe said it, then she would follow his every word. She underwent the massage therapy, but the decree had already been rendered.

On the morning of Sunday, 5 Adar I, Mother lost consciousness. That night, on the eve of 6 Adar I 5755/1995, she returned her pure soul to its Maker, with a *minyan* of her family and friends surrounding her bed.

Mother had departed from us to a world that is all good, leaving behind her a glorious family, generations of Torah scholars and *ovdei Hashem*; she had instructed all of us how to live a life for Hashem.

Her *aron* was taken to Eretz Yisrael, and she was buried in Tiveriah, alongside her husband, our father, the Sassover Rebbe, *zy"a*.

Her memory will never leave us, and we will never forget all that she taught us...

A LIFE OF JOY AND PRODUCTIVITY
WITH MY MOTHER, A"H

Rebbetzin Esther Rabinowitz, shetichyeh, speaks about her noble mother and a life of joy in her presence.

In retrospect, I wonder how my dear mother survived such a turbulent life.

Having had the privilege of growing up in her presence, everything looked normal, routine and smooth; I didn't sense that an exceptional life story was being played out in our home.

Mother gave us an elevated life, full of joy and positivity. She always saw the beautiful and good part of every situation, and opened our eyes to see the miracles of the Creator in His world. Despite all the suffering and troubles that were her lot, she did not allow fear or pessimism to gain a foothold in her life and her home. I don't remember the Holocaust accompanying her like a shadow; because we were so dear to her, she wanted us to enjoy the gift of life. She wasn't afraid for me to go on trips—on the contrary, she encouraged me to go out and see, to take in and enjoy the world.

Mother was a truly exceptional personality, a Rebbetzin in the full sense. Her heart burned with the constant desire to do more for the sake of Hashem, and she found creative ways to carry out her many ideas, all of which revolved around mitzvos and good deeds.

She was the one who, after my father's passing, managed the Yismach Moshe community. All the community's matters came to us; court hearings were routine for her, and she conducted negotiations with various companies, such as the Africa-Israel construction company.

To this day, all those who were in contact with her through her many activities remember her, and praise her personality and righteousness.

Her Connection to *Gedolei Yisrael*

Mother was deeply respected by *gedolei Yisrael*, who opened their doors to her whenever she came to seek advice or a *brachah*. Her children were also received very warmly by *gedolim* both in Eretz Yisrael and abroad.

In Eretz Yisrael, she would seek the advice of the Bais Yisrael of Ger, *zt"l*, before every step she took regarding raising the children, their *shidduchim* and their marriages; this continued with the Lev Simchah of Ger, *zt"l*, as well, and likewise for the Shefa Chaim of Sanz, *zt"l*, to whom my brother was very close, almost like a son, and the Machnovke Rebbe, *zt"l*.

In America, she was close to the Satmar Rebbe HaRav Yoel, *zt"l*, who was my father's uncle, and with whom we were also very close; the Rachmastrikve Rebbes, *zt"l*; the Bobover Rebbe, *zt"l*; *ybl"c* the Skulener Rebbe, *shlita*, the Skverer Rebbe, *shlita*, and numerous others, who always gave her precedence when it came an audience for *brachos* or advice. They respected her for everything that she symbolized as the Sassover Rebbetzin.

After Mother moved to Eretz Yisrael, as the widow of Reb Mordechai Pogromansky, the Miller family opened its doors to her and she came to live in their home.

HaRav Meir Miller, who had been close to Reb Mordechai, was appointed the chief rabbi of Bat Yam. He and his wife received an apartment that had one room and a hall. Mother stayed in the hall, and she would rise early, before her hosts, and go to sleep after them. While she was there, the Miller family grew, as two children were born, and Mother helped take care of them.

Mother never forgot the kindness of her benefactors, the Millers, and spoke often about their noble actions. Rebbetzin Miller, may she live many healthy years, is a dear aunt to us to this day.

Mother was one of the first bookkeepers in the diamond factory owned by the Goldfingers, near the Diamond Exchange. Her brilliance was outstanding; she simply had a computer brain. Years later, she could not understand why we relied on computers…

Ties with the Goldfinger family remain warm to this day. We are also grateful to them as they are generous supporters of Kollel Yismach Moshe.

While living in the Miller home, Mother heard about a relative of hers, a survivor who was not religious. She visited him and he told her that his aunt had survived the war, and he had married her in order to perpetuate the family that had been annihilated.

Mother recoiled. A Jew is not allowed to marry his aunt!

She didn't say a word during that visit. Like always, her mind controlled her emotions and she deliberated what to do: What was preferable? Perhaps it would be better for him to have sinned by accident and not intentionally? Even if she would apprise him of the prohibition involved in his marriage, it was hard to believe he would be convinced and break it up. After all, he wasn't observant; it would only make it worse because he would be intentionally transgressing a serious prohibition.

Mother exercised tremendous restraint in not expressing her distress over the situation. In her mind's eye was only one consideration: What did the Creator want from her at this moment? She gave no thought to her own feelings on the subject. She was the paragon of "*Bechol derachecha da'eihu!*"

When she returned from her relative's house, she relayed her dilemma to her host, Rav Miller. "That's a very difficult and crucial question. We have to ask the Chazon Ish," he said.

Mother went to the *posek hador* to ask. He did not usually accept women; they would write their question down on a note, give it to the *gabbai,* and he would give over the note to the Chazon Ish.

The *gabbai* brought mother's question to the Chazon Ish. He read it and asked, "Who is asking?"

"The widow of Reb Mordechai Pogromansky," the gabbai replied.

"*Eishes Chaver, kechaver.* Call her in," the *gaon* instructed.

Mother entered the Chazon Ish's room and he rose in respect, as he declared again, "*Eishes Chaver, kechaver!*"

Then he asked her to repeat the question. She told him the distressing information she had found out and wanted to know what to do: should she inform her relative that he was transgressing a serious sin, or would it be better if he did so without intending to?

The Chazon Ish went over to his bookcase, took out a Chumash, and opened to the *passuk* dealing with this issue. A distraught sigh emerged from his mouth as he closed the Chumash and said to Mother, "*Mit Yidden vos zenen dorch di Shoah, tchepet men nisht.*" One must not cause angst to Jews who went through the Holocaust.

"And what will be with the children who will be born?" Mother asked with concern.

"*HaKadosh Baruch Hu* has His ways," the Chazon Ish replied.

Mother emerged deeply awed by the Gadol Hador, and his sensitivity towards the survivors.

A short time later, one of the couple was killed in a car accident.

Mother related this story to us several times. She wanted to imbue us with the obligation to respect all *gedolei Yisrael* wherever they may be, from all the communities. In her eyes, they were all eminently holy.

She also told us that she had visited the Lubavitcher Rebbe, *zt"l*, and was present when dollars were distributed. The Rebbe would usually give each person one dollar, but he gave Mother a five dollar bill. Mother was very uncomfortable about this. After a few minutes, she returned and said, "I received a five dollar bill by mistake…this is not a single."

And the Rebbe replied, "That is for the children."

She had exactly five children.

The *Zechus*

Mother was eternally grateful to Hashem for having the privilege of being married to my father, the Sassover Rebbe, *zt"l*.

My parents lived in Yerushalayim for a short time after their marriage, and there, Mother met Golda. She knew Golda from the orphanage after the war; she was the girl who had been much smaller than the other girls her age.

Years had passed since Golda had married, but she had not yet been blessed with children. My mother urged her: "Listen to me, Golda! I married a great Rebbe. Come with your husband to get a *brachah* from him."

The couple came, and my father blessed them effusively. They merited a huge miracle and a short time later their first daughter was born.

Mother was so overjoyed that she had married and was able to perpetuate a continuation for her family that had been cut down. The children were born one after another, in America, and they were very energetic. My father was busy with his *avodas hakodesh*, learning in the *bais medrash*, ruling on *halachos* or *dinei Torah*. He was both a rav and a *dayan*, and Mother did not have it easy without any family members to help her.

That's where the wonderful Kosovitz family, who were neighbors, stepped in to help. It's impossible to describe what they did for us over the years, and may the *zechus* stand by them!

Mother tried to repay them as best she could. She taught the daughters geometry and algebra and other subjects. Even though she hadn't studied too much of these subjects herself, her brilliant mind helped her master any subject she chose. She also wrote songs and poems for the children for whichever purposes they needed. To this day, we remain in close contact with the Kosovitz family, and to us they are like extended family.

After my brother, Reb Shlomo, the Alesker Rebbe, *shlita*, was born, my father remarked to my mother, "We already have Shlomo, now we can have an Esther." Indeed, I was my parents' last child. My brother Shlomo was named for his great-grandfather, HaRav Shlomo of Sassov, *zy"a*, who my father still remembered.

My father served as the *mohel* at Shlomo's bris, but he was so emotional that he asked that another *mohel* stand alongside him. "I feel that this is the last bris we will be making," he said to my mother, which indeed it was.

With the Bais Yisrael of Ger

Mother was a very close friend of Rebbetzin Rochel Sarna, as mentioned earlier. They became friends when Reb Mordechai Pogromansky was ill and hospitalized in Switzerland. Rebbetzin Sarna was also there and she and mother became as close as sisters.

"Aunt Rochel" was our aunt, like Rebbetzin Miller was. There was also "Aunt Poriya," Mother's friend from the camps, and several other "aunts."

My father, *zt"l*, consulted the Bais Yisrael of Ger on various subjects that came up, including when he was sick.

While he lay so critically ill, my father sent Mother to the Bais Yisrael to seek advice on a specific matter. Mother came to the house on a Motzaei Shabbos after *Havdalah*. The *gabbai* was not there at the time and it was not possible to convey questions.

After she left, the Bais Yisrael learned that the Sassover Rebbetzin had been to the house. It was clear that if she had come, her question must have been urgent.

The following morning, on his daily walk, the Rebbe and his *meshamesh* went to Yeshivas Chevron on Hayeshivah Street. He sent the *gabbai* to call the *rosh yeshivah*, Rav Chaim Sarna, and when he emerged, the Rebbe said, "You surely know what the Sassover Rebbetzin wanted."

Rav Sarna was very agitated that the Rebbe had come all the way to him. "If the Rebbe wanted to speak to me, he could have sent the *gabbai* to summon me…"

Regarding Mother's question, Rav Sarna did not know. It was true that each time Mother came to the Gerrer Rebbe she would visit her friend, Rebbetzin Sarna, but this time, she had not done so.

The Rebbe replied, "Please let the Rebbetzin know that I'll be back at lunchtime and she can convey the question."

Mother was summoned and arrived at the appointed time at the Sarna home, right near Yeshivas Chevron. A few moments later, the Rebbe's figure could be seen approaching, with his *meshamesh*.

The question was asked in a most interesting fashion: The Rebbe and his *gabbai* stood on one side of the street, while Mother and Rebbetzin Sarna stood on the other side. The *gabbai* asked Mother what she wanted to ask, and then returned to the Rebbe and conveyed the question. He heard the Rebbe's answer and crossed the street again with a response. This went back and forth a few times until Mother had her answer.

While my father was hospitalized in Hadassah Hospital, the Gerrer Rebbe visited him each week; he also came to the house in Kiryas Yismach Moshe occasionally.

There were times when my father was conscious, and times that he wasn't. Once, when he lay unconscious, the Rebbe came to visit. One of the people in the room dared to ask the Rebbe, "The Sassover Rebbe does not know or see who comes to visit."

The Rebbe replied that it was also important to give *chizuk* to the Rebbetzin.

Before his passing, my father expressed a request that the Bais Yisrael be the custodian over his children. Indeed, after his passing, our mother would send questions to the Rebbe regarding every matter of *chinuch* and raising the children.

The Rebbe treated my brother in a fatherly manner. When the children of the Sassover Rebbe came, the doors opened and they were allowed into the Rebbe's room, sometimes even for ten minutes at a time. The Rebbe would ask them questions about their lives and heard them out with great compassion.

A Memorial to the First Rebbetzin

My mother was married to my father for ten and a half years, the last two years of which he was largely bedridden and suffering. During the nine healthy years, my father spent a lot of time in Eretz Yisrael establishing Kiryas Yismach Moshe, while Mother remained alone in America raising the children.

Nevertheless, wondrously, Mother imparted to us the legacy of our holy ancestors of the Sassover dynasty, as though she had lived with my father for many years and knew his forbears personally. With her brilliant mind, she remembered the fine details of everyone's *yichus*, including dates and remarkable stories. Orphaned of our father, we grew up with these stories, which were both a privilege and an obligation at the same time.

Mother also frequently mentioned our father's first wife, Rebbetzin Chaya Roisa, the daughter of the Satmar Rebbe Rav Yoel *zt"l*. She told us of her piety, as our father had told her (my father and his first wife were cousins). It appeared as though Mother had known the Rebbetzin personally!

In order to ensure that the Rebbetzin's memory was preserved,

Mother asked us, her children, to name children after her. Indeed, each of her children named one of their daughters Chaya Roisa.

For the first month of their marriage, our parents stayed at the Reich Hotel in Yerushalayim. Once, while sitting in the garden of the hotel, they noticed a Jew with an aristocratic bearing nervously pacing back and forth. They approached the man and asked why he seemed so sad.

"My name is Moshe Pardo. I arranged a meeting here with a philanthropist in order to establish the Ohr HaChaim institutions for girls from Sephardic backgrounds, but the meeting didn't work out," the man replied sadly. Mother turned to my father and said, "Perhaps we should donate towards Ohr HaChaim, in memory of Rebbetzin Chaya Roisa, your first wife…"

My father heeded her advice and he was the one who gave a contribution for the first building of Mosdos Ohr HaChaim. Rebbetzin Chaya Roisa's name was commemorated on the building.

We felt free to speak with Mother about our father, and every so often we asked her questions without feeling the slightest bit uncomfortable. For example, we asked, "When Mashiach comes, who will he go back to, you or his first wife? Because it says that at *techiyas hameisim*, each person will return to the wife of his youth, or the wife who bore him children. So where will our father go?"

"That's an interesting question," she replied simply. "We'll have to wait and see!"

Don't Forget Our Father

A large, almost life-sized, picture of our father, hung in an inside room in our home. It was a nearly tangible image and it was as if he was there with us.

Mother wisely hung the picture so that we should remember him. I, who became an orphan at the age of three and a half, remember him because of this picture.

When he passed away on 11 Adar, our kindergarten in Yismach Moshe was getting ready for the Purim party. Mother, who was sitting *shivah*, asked that I be dressed in my costume. Those around her said, "It's not right. The family is sitting *shivah* and the girl will have a party in kindergarten as though nothing happened?"

But Mother replied, "Esty will be an orphan for the rest of her life. Now she has no obligation of *aveilus*."

This was the realistic outlook that she applied to every area her life, and she did not allow herself or her children to be swept up in painful emotions.

After preschool, I began to attend the elementary school in our community. We became very close to the principal, Mrs. Sarah Nankenski and were almost like family. When Mrs. Nankenski once made a bris on Shabbos, Mother walked from Yismach Moshe to Bnei Brak to participate in her *simchah*.

One day, the principal found me standing at the window gazing out at the pouring rain.

"What are you thinking about, Esty?" she asked gently.

I shared my feelings. "It's raining and my father is getting wet."

The wonderful principal shared this with my mother so she should know what kind of thoughts were passing through my mind...

Mother sat down beside me and consoled me with explanations that would calm me.

With aplomb, she was able to maneuver between our difficulties.

I really lacked for nothing. Mother was both a father and mother figure to us. She had a very strong personality and always gave us her support.

She even learned Gemara with my brothers! She was extremely knowledgeable and immediately grasped what the Gemara was saying.

Each week, she visited the yeshivos where my brothers learned. She would speak to the *rosh yeshivah* and the *mashgiach* about how her son was progressing in his learning and *Yiras Shamayim*, and thus filled the role of both father and mother, as she was destined to do from Above.

A Home of Holiness and Greatness

We had the privilege of growing up in a home of holiness; from the time our father became ill until the marriage of my oldest brother, the *bais medrash* was housed in our spacious home.

Mother infused us with love for the *mikdash me'at*, and explained what a *zechus* it was for us to be able to honor the House of Hashem. There was always an elevated atmosphere at home because of the *bais medrash,* and it obligated us children to behave properly; to dress, speak and act in a way that befitted those who dwell in the house of the King. In general, Mother always expected us to act with refinement, and she never allowed us to utter even a single word that was not clean and dignified. Each Friday, a young man would come to the house, open the *sefer Torah* and read the *parshah* to ensure there were no mistakes. The pleasant tune was literally music to our ears...

Mother had special ways to mark each approaching Yom Tov. On Erev Shavuos she would go with us to pick flowers and then she sat with us as we created a chain of roses that we used to adorn the *sefer Torah*. We also decorated the house to look like Har Sinai; on Shavuos night, the shul was filled with dozens of people learning Torah, singing pleasantly as they learned. It was a remarkable spiritual experience that was deeply ingrained in the children, and the *niggunim* accompany us to this day.

We loved the shul so much that on Hoshanah Rabbah, we would argue amongst ourselves about who would get to sweep out the shul after the banging of the *hoshanos*.

Purim was like Yom Kippur for Mother, a day of pleas and prayers, awe and intensity. At the same time, she never forgot anyone when it came to sending Mishloach Manos. She sent to the entire family, every acquaintance and many unfortunate people that she knew.

Every mitzvah, every Yom Tov, was an entire "Torah" for Mother. She kept the *minhagim* with tremendous awe, living them and infusing us with the sublime spirit of tradition.

Courage that Crossed Borders

Mother's personality was a unique combination of refinement, modesty, and reserve, while at the same time she was infused with strength and courage to do what was necessary. An example of this latter trait was her frequent clandestine flights to Communist Poland.

My mother had an aunt who lived in Krakow with her daughter (the one who hid Rivka'le for a few weeks during the war, and where Mother stayed for a time after the war.)

The aunt and her daughter had taken on gentile identities during the war, and after the war was over they elected to maintain their Polish identities, for fear of returning to the long-suffering Jewish nation. The two did not deny their faith; they appreciated religion, but they were paralyzed by fear, and this prevented them from reverting back to their original lifestyle.

Remarkably, the year the war ended, a priest came to their home and informed them, "I know that you are Jews—and so you should know that tomorrow is Yom Kippur!"

All Mother's efforts to persuade her aunt and her cousin to leave Poland were in vain. The daughter had juvenile diabetes and they feared they would not manage in the big, intimidating world. Perhaps the weather would have a detrimental effect on her...and maybe...and perhaps...They came up with all kinds of "reasons" why it was better for them to stay where they were.

When our parents lived in America, the aunt wrote Mother in a letter that she was not managing with the Polish insulin. At the time, Poland was under Communist rule, and sending packages behind the Iron Curtain was virtually impossible. Mother, in her wisdom, contacted an American priest and was able to send insulin to Poland for her cousin through the church!

This arrangement lasted for years.

After we moved to Eretz Yisrael, Mother traveled once every two or three years to visit her aunt and her daughter—for a single day each time! It was a very dangerous trip, not unlike entering the lion's den. For the duration of the trip we had no contact with Mother; from when she entered Poland and until she left, we didn't know what was happening to her in that country that was so hostile to Jews.

No one was allowed to know she was a Jew, because she could be imprisoned or put to death for the fact alone. That's why she would fly to several countries en route to her real destination.

The route began in Eretz Yisrael. From there, she flew to the United States and replaced her American passport so that the Polish officials should not see the Israeli stamps. From there, she traveled to Poland as an American tourist, and made sure to speak only fluent English while she was there (she had taught herself English).

She always traveled during the winter so that she could cover her head with a hat that would not invite questions. She was careful not to disclose her Polish origins, because that could also cause complications. The Poles were afraid to start up with the Americans so as not to trigger a diplomatic flare up.

What did Mother do on that one day every few years that she spent in her aunt's house in Poland?

First of all, she brought her aunt a Jewish calendar so she would know when the Jewish holidays fell. Throughout the year, Mother photographed us at every opportunity doing Jewish things, such as lighting Chanukah candles. When she visited her aunt she would show them the photos so that she and her daughter could see what Jewish life was like and get a taste of Yiddishkeit. She also gave them chocolate and sugarless candies, items they could not obtain in Poland. Mother brought lots of pairs of socks, which didn't weigh much, for her aunt to sell on the black market.

The constant connection Mother made sure to maintain ensured that the two women would not be totally cut off from the Jewish nation.

Mother would land at the airport in Warsaw, and from there she would take an internal flight to Krakow. She would then travel back to Warsaw, and on to America.

She once had a very powerful, inspiring experience at the airport:

Mother was waiting at Warsaw's small, shabby airport when she heard an announcement that the flights were being delayed

He had many talmidim, and his image accompanied them throughout their lives.

The Sassover Rebbe, *zt"l*, as a young man.

I felt that I had to build a true life of Torah! A life that would express my tremendous gratitude to HaKadosh Baruch Hu for being with me throughout the Holocaust and keeping me alive.

The Sassover Rebbe, *zt"l*.

The Rebbetzin *z"l* 5737

"Why did only I remain alive from my entire family?" I would often ask the Rebbe.
"You have to understand," he explained to me — and I never tired of hearing it —*"we can see clearly that it was decreed from Above that specifically you should be the mother of Yosef Dovid, Henoch, Moshe'le, Shloime'le, and Esther."*

The Sassover Rebbe and Rebbetzin, *zy"a*, with their sons, *shlita*, in America.

234

My parents never abandoned their dream of returning to Eretz Yisrael.

The Rebbe, *zt"l*, during meetings regarding the establishment of Kiryas Yismach Moshe in Eretz Yisrael.

We remained alone, five little children, under the care of the babysitter. During Aseres Yemei Teshuvah *we traveled to Eretz Yisrael.*

The five children in the airport in America, en route to Eretz Yisrael, after their father became sick, and their mother had traveled ahead of them to take care of him.

The Rebbe during *sandakaus*. At right is his devoted *gabbai*, Reb Yeshayah Itzkowitz, *z"l*.

235

The Rebbe inserting the *kvittel* in the ground while pouring the cornerstone for Kiryas Yismach Moshe.

At the cornerstone laying ceremony of Kiryas Yismach Moshe, during the speeches. From Right to Left: HaRav Yaakov Landa, Rav and Av Bais Din of Bnei Brak, *zt"l*; the Koidenover Rebbe, *zt"l*, a relative and close friend of the Rebbe; Ashkenazi Chief Rabbi, Rav Unterman, *zt"l*; the Sassover Rebbe, *zt"l*; the Sephardic Chief Rabbi HaRav Yitzchak Nissim, *zt"l*; and the Modzhitzer Rebbe, *zt"l*.

236

Standing beside Israel's chief rabbis at the cornerstone-laying of Kiryas Yismach Moshe.

During the signing ceremony for the purchase of the land for Kiryas Yismach Moshe. Sitting on the left of the Rebbe is the Boyaner Rebbe, *zt"l*, of America. On the left side of the photo is the Rebbe's brother, HaRav Yoel Teitelbaum, the Kirelhauser Rebbe, *zt"l*.

A meeting to discuss Kiryas Yismach Moshe. Second from the right, standing, is Mr. Baruch Duvdevani, *z"l*, the secretary general of the Jewish Agency, a Jew with a heart of gold—and a descendant of HaRav Elimelech of Lizhensk, who greatly helped *gedolei Yisrael* obtain funding to establish chareidi Jewry in Eretz Yisrael.

due to heavy storms. The passengers would be put up at a hotel.

Every pair of passengers received one room. Mother asked to be placed with a woman, and she was paired up with a Polish student in her thirties who was planning to leave the country to visit the big wide world. As they sat together they got into conversation.

Mother was a fascinating conversationalist, and found a common language with everyone. The most scholarly person could spend hours in riveting conversation with her; she was proficient in the histories of many nations, and for example, could recite the names of all the presidents of the United States and which years they served.

By contrast, even the the hired cleaning help felt comfortable around her, as though she was their good friend. She gave everyone she spoke to the feeling that they were valuable to her, and she was never conceited.

Mother and the Polish student spoke for hours. Mother waited for the moment the other woman would go to sleep; after all, she had to *daven* Maariv, and she could not have the gentile woman see her praying—it would betray her Jewish identity...

At the time, Mother *davened* three *tefillos* a day.

In the years when she cared for her young children, my father told her, "A mother of young children is not obligated in *tefillah*; but you should always say a *perek* or two of Tehillim."

When the children grew up a bit, she *davened* Shacharis, Minchah, and Maariv. She also finished the entire *sefer Tehillim* before *davening* without stopping to speak, which is known as a *segulah*. In her final twenty years, she completed *sefer Tehillim* twice a day, once in the morning without stopping to speak, and the other during the day, when she would say a few *perakim* whenever she had a chance.

Now she faced a dilemma. She could recite *Kriyas Shema* under her blanket, but by *davening Shemoneh Esrei*, she risked giving herself away. Communism reigned supreme in Poland,

FOREVER IN FAITH • 239

and there was a lot of fear. As such, hiding her true identity was a matter of *pikuach nefesh*!

On the other hand, how could she forego the *tefillah* she *davened* each night?

Thoughts raced through her mind, with arguments in favor of each option…Finally, she came to a decision: she could not forego her custom just because of a gentile woman!

"Excuse me," she told her roommate. "Before I go to sleep, I have to recite something." And she stood in the corner of the room and *davened*.

When Mother *davened*, she was like a soldier before her Commander. She *davened* with solemnity and fear, and stood motionless as she spoke to her Creator.

Mother was always a reserved, regal, and aristocratic woman, but we knew that inside, there were wellsprings of emotion that were manifested primarily in her written poems and songs. When I was away from home, I loved receiving her letters, which were overflowing with love. But in day-to-day life, it was her mind that controlled her heart. It is likely that this trait is what helped her survive the Holocaust and overcome the many challenges life presented her in subsequent years.

Through her pure *tefillos* she merited great *siyata diShmaya*. She had a "direct line" with Hashem, and to Rabi Shimon Bar Yochai. When she waited for a bus, she would ask simply, "Reb Shimon, a hitch," and the bus arrived within moments.

Whenever we needed something we would say, "Mother, ask Reb Shimon for a ride…"

Mother stood and *davened* to her Creator in the Communist lion's den, and she felt the gentile woman's eyes boring into her back the entire time.

She began to feel afraid, and hesitated: should she continue or finish? Who knew what was waiting for her when she took three steps back?

Having no choice, she finished her *tefillah*...and then the gentile woman asked, "What were you doing?"

Having no other choice, Mother replied, "I believe in the Creator of the world!"

The woman looked at her strangely. "What do you mean, you believe? And who is the Creator?"

Mother spent the rest of the night explaining to the gentile woman Who the Creator was and the meaning of faith. They never even went to sleep! In a pleasant, understandable way, Mother explained these concepts to the non-Jewish woman, who was so far removed from the very idea. Throughout the night, she fearfully awaited the moment the woman would turn hostile.

In the morning, before they returned to the airport, the woman blurted out to Mother, "I envy you..."

The Hatzolah Representative

Mother was a refined Rebbetzin, with *Yiras Shamayim*; she was a wonderful *eishes chayil* and was also a very active, accomplished person. It would be impossible to detail all the things she was involved in. She helped disseminate Torah and her *chessed* was boundless. Some dubbed her "Mrs. Thatcher" because, with her remarkable character traits and strengths, she reminded them of the British prime minister.

Mother bore the heavy burden of Yismach Moshe, which was a contracting company in the full sense of the word. There were constantly meetings with company executives and business people in our home, and she often attended court hearings and dealt with lawyers and accountants.

At one point, Yismach Moshe was in financial difficulties

and on the verge of bankruptcy. During that time, Mother sold assets to Africa-Israel.

With tremendous gratitude, this is the place to mention the eminent Rabbi Shlomo Mishkovsky, *z"l*, a *talmid chacham* and a very special person, who got involved at this difficult time.

Rabbi Mishkovsky was an accountant from Tel Aviv. After the passing of my father, when the company encountered a severe crisis, Rebbetzin Rochel Sarna suggested that Rabbi Mishkovsky take things into his hands, and indeed, he did so. He was assisted by Mrs. Esther Burstein, who continued to work dedicatedly for him for more than forty years.

Rabbi Mishkovsky was able to pull the carriage out of the mud, so to speak, and the company paid all its debts to suppliers. He continued to oversee the company, providing advice throughout. May this be a *zechus* for him and his family.

Until the sale of those assets, our financial situation was dire. We literally couldn't afford to buy bread. One day, electric company workers came to cut off our electricity.

Mother went out into the stairwell and spoke to the electric company representative: "I just wanted you to know that I am a widow with five children. Right now I don't have any means to pay, but *b'ezras Hashem* I will. If that is your job, do what they tell you. I just wanted you to know…"

The man took pity on Mother and he left without cutting off the electricity.

The cups in our house were empty *leben* containers. We would rinse them out and use them over and over again because there wasn't enough money to purchase real cups! We were rambunctious, lively children, and the cups broke one after another; the empty *leben* containers were an ideal solution.

We didn't feel disadvantaged at all. When my friends asked why we drank out of empty *leben* cups, I explained to them what my mother had told me: "The regular cups break so fast. Isn't it a shame? When we'll grow up, we'll buy real cups."

Mother always saw the good in everything and the positive points in every person. She never spoke badly of anyone.

As part of her job as the director of Yismach Moshe, there were times when people caused her aggravation, but she didn't speak badly of them. On the contrary, she would help them in all kinds of remarkable ways.

Once a complainant showed up at our house and began to shout loudly; at one point he started throwing chairs. I, as a little girl, was terrified.

Mother held my hand and took me down to one of our devoted neighbors. She asked the neighbor to take us in and lock the door. She waited there with me until we heard the man go down the stairs.

"Poor man," Mother said. "He lost control of himself, which is why he behaved like he did," she defended him.

A short time later, the man came to ask Mother's forgiveness. She moved on, without making a fuss over the incident.

Another person would aggravate her constantly. In time, he needed financial assistance in order to marry off his daughter, and my mother secretly raised money for the *kallah* so she could get married with dignity.

Mother was a role model for *hachnassas orchim*. People of all kinds would come to our home, including those who were not bestowed with an abundance of common sense. They felt very *"heimish"* and during *davening*, or during breaks such as *krias haTorah*, they would come in, open the refrigerator, take out whatever food they found, and eat heartily...

Sometimes Mother would hide the delicacies in a different refrigerator in the apartment next door, but they somehow got there as well and ate our food. It bothered us children, but Mother would soothe us and explain, "Even if they don't know how to act, *we* have to have good *middos*."

Mother found a way to speak to each person on his level. She was brilliant and picked up languages such as Moroccan and Italian, so she was able to warmly encourage and support new immigrants from Morocco who lived in Ganei Tikva, right near Yismach Moshe. They were honored to be in the company of the respected Rebbetzin; they were captivated by her honesty, openness, clarity, and friendliness.

The Robbery

Mother sensed what was in the offing and sometimes dreamt about things that were going to happen. Here are a few exceptional examples:

While I was a young girl, Mother traveled abroad every so often to raise funds for the *kollel*, sometimes remaining for long periods of time to receive treatment. I mostly stayed at the home of my brother, the Rebbe, in Kiryas Yismach Moshe.

Mother made sure I didn't feel at all like a *nebach*. When she returned home for *Yamim Tovim* or *simchahs*, she was always loaded down with gifts. During the summers, I traveled abroad to camp, which I thoroughly enjoyed and of which I have many fond memories.

An orphaned *bochur* slept in our large, empty house when we were gone. One day, Mother called my brother, the Rebbe, and said worriedly, "Rebbe (that's how she addressed him), what's with the robbery?"

My brother, who lived across the street, did not understand. "Which robbery?"

"Tell me. Don't be afraid. I know there was a robbery," Mother said with certainty.

But the Rebbe truly didn't know about anything. "I don't know. There was no robbery."

"Go up to the house now and check!" she asked. "I dreamed that there was a robbery at home!"

My brother called the house and asked the *bochur*, "Yitzchak, what's doing?"

"Everything's fine," the *bochur* replied, puzzled.

"Can you see if everything's okay in the apartment? The Rebbetzin says she dreamed that there was a robbery," the Rebbe requested.

Yitzchak checked the house through and through and saw that everything was in place; nothing had happened.

My brother called Mother and reported that everything was in order.

The next night, there was a break-in. Mother was supposed to return the following day.

During the evening of the robbery, Yitzchak called my brother. "Rebbe, why are people bothering me? The phone keeps ringing and the caller hangs up!"

It turns out that the thieves were trying to check who was home and how many people were there. The next day, we discovered that all the silver had been stolen. These were extremely valuable items; we had a lot of precious silver, some of which had been passed down from generations before the Holocaust.

My brother, the Rebbe, immediately called the police; the scene could not be touched until the police came so that fingerprints would not be damaged. He asked the police to come as fast as possible because the Rebbetzin was scheduled to return, and the house had to be restored to order before she arrived.

For some reason, it took the police some time to come, and Mother arrived while the house was still in the chaotic state the thieves had left in their wake.

At the airport, we told her there *had* been a robbery and the house was a big mess. She took the news calmly because she'd already been emotionally prepared by her dream. But we were extremely agitated.

The next day, a detective came to the house. Mother listed for him the items that had been stolen, describing each piece in detail. The detective marveled at Mother's sharp memory and descriptive abilities.

Mother was very pained by the robbery. Those holy items were very dear to my father, and their disappearance meant that a part of him had been taken from the house. The items that had been stolen were valued at about fifty thousand dollars, in those days.

Police made every effort to track down the thieves. Ultimately, they were able to nab them, and made a deal to have all the items returned. The silver had been buried in an orchard behind our house (today the Maccabit Road), and were still wrapped in the sheet the thieves had stripped off one of the beds.

The police were very pleased that the thieves had been apprehended and the items were returned. They took photos with the silver and with our family, and we were overjoyed that the story had a happy ending, *baruch Hashem*.

Alone in an Arab Area

The phone rang in my brother, the Rebbe's house; it was Mother on the line from America. "What's doing with Esther? Is she taking care of herself? Is she alright?" she fretted.

That day, I had gone on a trip to Tiveriah with two friends, and we stayed at the Florida Hotel, managed by the Luria family. During the day, we joined a group that was also staying at the hotel for a trip. In the evening, we got separated from the group, and we were stuck in an Arab area of Haifa.

We were three girls alone, and it was dark out; all around us were Arabs...

We stood frightened and at a loss.

Suddenly, a police car stopped and we quickly piled inside, seeking shelter from the hostile surroundings. To our surprise, we found two Gerrer *chassidim*, police volunteers, in the car. They asked what brought us to this area.

We told them that we had been separated from our group and that we had to return to the hotel in Tiveriah. They tried to find a bus that would take us to Tiveriah, but could not, and therefore, we remained in Haifa for the night, as the guests of one of the volunteers and his family.

And Mother sensed all this!

The Nice Side of Life

When Mother became sick with her eye ailment, it became necessary to extract her eye and replace it with an artificial one. The surgery was done in America, and first, a temporary artificial eye was implanted, followed later by a permanent one that closely resembled a natural eye.

I was very interested in art at the time. Mother wrote me in her letters, "Esther, I miss you here. You would so enjoy to see the work that the experts do here at the hospital to prepare the eye; it's literally a work of art! You would be so impressed at their precision, how they blend the colors...I am sure you would like to see this kind of art."

Her letters were always upbeat; that's how she turned the treatment of her disease into something artistic that she could marvel at…

In her final illness, we were sent to Texas to treat her liver. The doctor there was an Israeli, a graduate of Hadassah, who remembered my father when he was a patient in Yerushalayim.

This is the place to note the exceptional devotion of my sister-in-law, Rebbetzin Chana Mindel Teitelbaum, *a"h*, who passed away a few years ago from a serious illness. It is impossible to describe the way she cared for Mother. She was the one who was in touch with the doctors and accompanied Mother to the hospital in Texas, so far from her own home.

My sister-in-law, who had a small baby at the time, purchased a special folding infant seat for the trip. She left her house, with her baby, in order to travel with Mother to the hospital, where she remained for the duration of the hospitalization, which entailed both tests and the treatment. After Mother's first surgery, it was only natural that she should rest in the home of my sister-in-law's mother, her *mechuteiniste*, Rebbetzin Geldzahler, *a"h* (who passed away on Rosh Chodesh Kislev 5770), the daughter of of Rav Eliyahu Dessler, *zt"l*. She cared for Mother with outstanding devotion and graciousness.

The hospital where Mother was treated was in Houston, near the Space Center. Mother knew that her illness was terminal. At first, she preferred not to treat it, thinking it was a waste of money that she preferred to pass on to the children. Later she decided that she couldn't die without knowing that she had done her best. A person has to make the effort and the key to life is in the Hands of Hashem.

On the way to the doctor in Houston, we took her to the Space Center to show her the shuttles. "To be so close to where they are and not to visit would really be missing an opportunity!" Mother claimed. Despite her condition, she asked us to take her so she could see the miraculous achievements of mankind and take photos in the space ships.

Mother lived the rest of her life with joy and a positive attitude, and had the merit to be independent and not reliant on others until her final day.

She always told me that she asked Hashem that the merit of the Tehillim that she recited each day should spare her from having to be a burden to others. She had seen our father, in his most serious condition, when he required assistance, and she *davened* fervently that no one should have to care for her like that. Indeed, despite her serious illnesses, she walked unaided until her final day.

Throughout the years, I wanted Mother to write down her memories. Her emotions were much more evident in her writing; when she spoke, she did so in a restrained, composed manner—a trait that helped her overcome so many difficult challenges in her life.

For that very reason, she had trouble writing down her memories. It was hard for her to face the overwhelming emotions of her Holocaust experiences that roiled inside her like stormy seas. The notebook and pen I prepared for her remained in their spot in the kitchen, untouched...

On Tishah B'Av, when she was at the home of my brother, the Sassov-Monsey Rebbe, *shlita*, she began to speak, and her words were preserved on tape. That was the beginning of the story she ultimately recorded in increments over the next few weeks.

Her Final Days

Three weeks before her passing, Mother flew to Eretz Yisrael to participate in the bar mitzvah of her grandson, Rav Yochanan Teitelbaum, the son of my brother, the Alesker Rebbe, Rav Shlomo, *shlita*. Although her condition was critical and she could hardly walk, she refused to miss the *simchah*.

At the same time, my neighbor's husband passed away, leaving her a widow with young children. Mother spoke to this neighbor by phone for hours, offering encouragement and support; she shared her own experiences of raising children without a husband and father; about the Divine mission and the strength one receives from Above. She continued speaking until she felt that she had infused the widow with the strength to take on the task ahead of her.

The widow, encouraged from her words, was unaware of Mother's dire condition.

Three weeks later, this neighbor spoke to me, her grief and admiration both apparent: "I didn't dream for a moment that when the Rebbetzin spoke to me she was literally on her deathbed…She spoke so calmly and gave me so much *koach*. Where did it come from?!"

Mother spent her final days in the home of the Kosovitz family in America. She repeatedly said, "They are calling me, they are calling me…" Evidently, the souls of her loved ones were calling to her from Above, as they waited for the arrival of her precious soul, which had established future generations to perpetuate her glorious family.

One day, Mother spoke to the non-Jewish woman in the house, from her bed. "Please open the window; I want to see who is calling me."

The gentile woman recoiled and hurried to tell Mrs. Kosovitz that the angel of death was in the house…She was afraid to be alone with Mother in the room!

After that, Mother no longer said that anyone was calling her.

She wasn't at all afraid of death. She rejoiced as her final day approached because she had prepared a huge "package" of mitzvos and good deeds to take with her; throughout her life she had constantly overcome obstacles that rose up before her.

On Motzaei Shabbos *Parshas Terumah* she ate Melavah Malkah. On Sunday morning she woke up, said *Modeh Ani*, and washed her hands, but when she got out of bed, she suddenly lost consciousness. She was taken to the hospital.

That evening, the eve of 6 Adar I, she passed away in holiness and purity.

More than a *minyan* of relatives stood around her bed and tearfully recited *Nishmas, Kriyas Shema, Viduy,* and *pesukei yichud.* We felt a tremendous *zechus* to escort our holy mother, who had reached her final destination after such a tumultuous journey, and to be in the presence of her purified soul that was rising On High to take its place together with the souls of pious women from throughout the generations.

Tehei nafsha tzerurah bitzror hachaim; zchusah tagen aleinu.

CHAYCHIE

Rebbetzin Esther Rabinowitz commemorates a dear soul while speaking of the wellsprings of chessed and love that flowed from her mother's heart, and about her strength of spirit and bitachon. These are things that cannot be quantified, that have no boundaries...

They came together to the orphanage in Aix-les-Bains, survivors of the inferno, two girls alone in the world who bonded with each other. One was Chaychie (her real name), and the other was Leah'le (a pseudonym).

Mother knew Chaychie from Tarnow; she was a friend of one of Mother's older sisters. As a counselor in Aix-les-Bains, Mother was very devoted to the two friends and provided for them both materially and spiritually (even though they were older than she was), as did Mother's friend, Rebbetzin Miller. Slowly, most of the girls left the orphanage as they were adopted by families or married and built their own homes. Many of the girls traveled to Eretz Yisrael and other countries around the world.

Around that time, it became apparent that Leah'le was sick with muscular dystrophy and would never be able to have a family. Chaychie, on the other hand, was an intelligent, talented girl with sterling *middos*. She had a prestigious lineage, going back to the Chozeh of Lublin. Until the war, she had grown up in a respected, affluent home. Her entire family was annihilated.

Chaychie had everything going for her and could have chosen any *shidduch* from a number of very distinguished suggestions.

But Chaychie pitied poor Leah'le, and devoted herself to caring for her. Leah'le became entirely dependent on Chaychie. When suitable *shidduch* suggestions were made, Leah'le would explain to Chaychie why it was not good enough for her.

Thus, Chaychie and Leah'le remained tied to one another. The girls all dispersed, each finding a new path in life, while these two remained alone with nowhere to go.

The French government took custody of the two refugees and gave them French citizenship. The welfare authorities took responsibility for them and arranged for monetary compensation from Germany.

The kibbutz in Aix-les-Bains closed and the two moved to a French old-age home. They were assigned a room, which became their home. We cannot imagine how two young refugees, alone in the world, one of them sick with a degenerative disease, possibly felt living in a gentile old-age home.

Two families cared for the girls: the family of the *rosh hakahal* in France, Rabbi Lederberger, and Rabbi Moshe Lebel and his wife, Rachel, who lived in Paris. They would periodically visit the two girls to see how they were faring. With great devotion, they took care of their needs and served as an address where they could turn.

Years passed, and Chaychie and Leah'le spent their days in the old-age home. Chaychie, who was talented and had very good taste, began to work as a seamstress at upscale salons.

Chaychie devoted most of her time and energy to caring for her sick friend. Leah'le's muscular dystrophy grew steadily more severe and Chaychie spared no effort to make her more comfortable.

Over the years, Mother would visit them at the old age home. When she flew from Eretz Yisrael to America in order to collect money for the *kollel* in Yismach Moshe or for treatments, she would make a stop in France so she could visit them.

It was sort of a "living will" that the survivors felt obligated to uphold: we were sisters in times of trouble and sisters we will remain. We have to continue worrying for each other for the rest of our lives! The survivors were especially concerned about the lone people who never established families, and felt an unwavering sense of obligation toward them.

I remember myself as a little girl, hearing Mother speak on the phone worriedly: "What happened to Chaychie and Leah'le? Why is there no contact with them? I haven't heard from them for a long time!"

The Lederberger and Lebel families in France updated Mother that the two were simply not opening their door at the old-age home!

Again and again they knocked, but there was no answer or any sound from inside. Finally, the Lederbergers decided there was no choice but to break the door down. The police were summoned, the door was broken down, and the two were found inside the room—alive, well, and fully aware of their surroundings.

Leah'le's muscular dystrophy had apparently been compounded by paranoia, and she was convinced she was constantly being pursued. She trembled in fear, thinking that the Germans had come to take her to the camps. In order to prevent that from happening, she locked the door to be safe. She swept Chaychie up in fears of the impending arrival of the Nazis, and the two preferred to live behind a locked door.

"Straight to the hospital!" the police ordered when they heard this. They took the two girls, one healthy and one sick, to the hospital.

Once there, Leah'le and Chaychie received medications and drugs and even electric shocks. That's how the French treated two wretched survivors—by drugging them.

The authorities continued to receive the compensation from Germany for the two survivors and transferred the money to the old-age home, where the girls were registered. The director of the nursing home gave them as much money as he saw fit to cover their needs.

Mother and her worried friends were in constant contact by mail and telephone. Mother, the Lederbergers and the Lebels made every effort to persuade the hospital management to release them. In the meantime, poor, ailing Leah'le passed away.

Just around then, Chaychie fell and broke her pelvis. She was treated and then returned to live in the old-age home alone. On Shabbos she would be a guest of either the Lederbergers or the Lebels. Every so often she was hosted by the families of two *tzaddikim*, HaRav Itzikel of Pshevorsk and the Av Bais Din of Strasbourg, *zt"l*.

Chaychie continued to live under French custodianship, and she was forbidden to leave the country. She wasn't her own person; she was overseen by the welfare department and was legally dependent.

The years that Chaychie had spent in the presence of sick people, the drugs and the medications she had been forced to take, in addition to five and a half horrific Holocaust years, took a toll on Chaychie's emotional state. She became extremely suspicious and lived with the feeling that the whole world was out to get her, and that the Germans would be arriving imminently to take her away.

Mother invested extensive efforts until she was able, with the help of the two noble French families, to persuade the authorities to allow Chaychie out of the country for a visit to Eretz Yisrael. It was a slow, complicated process, but the efforts eventually bore fruit. The friends split the cost of the ticket, and Mother took upon herself to host the guest.

Mother was a widow with young children to care for, and was very busy both in and out of the home, with her obligations as a Rebbetzin as well as with the many acts of *chessed* she did. The burden of managing Yismach Moshe also rested on her shoulders. Nevertheless, she dedicated herself to the project of bringing Chaychie to Eretz Yisrael. She was the contact person with the Lederbergers, and they liaised with the authorities and obtained the permits from the social worker, the custodian, the judge, and others. Mother took responsibility to ensure that Chaychie would be well cared for and would return to France promptly.

The Miller family volunteered to host Chaychie during the week, when Mother was so busy. On Shabbos and *Yamim Tovim*, she would come to our house.

The day after Yom Kippur, we traveled to the airport to welcome Chaychie and bring her home with us.

Thus began a new chapter in Chaychie's life. She loved being in Eretz Yisrael, among fellow Jews. In our house, she was accorded royal treatment! "Chaychie is very, very important," Mother explained to us. "She comes from a very prestigious *yichus* and I am asking you to treat her with the respect she deserves."

We perceived Chaychie as a martyr who gave up her own life for others. We had so much compassion for her and gave her whatever she needed and wanted, but she hardly demanded anything. She had a very aristocratic bearing, manifest, among other ways, in her long silences.

Mother wanted her to look good so she sent her to have her hair dyed. As a teenager, I accompanied her to the hairdresser in Petach Tikva.

While the hairdresser was doing her work, she asked Chaychie what her name was.

"Weinberg," Chaychie replied laconically.

That was all we needed...

All the way home from Petach Tikva to Kiryas Yismach Moshe, Chaychie kept asking me fearfully: "Why did she ask me my name? She wants to tell the Germans that I'm here; she's going to inform them. Why would she care what my name is? Why did she ask me?"

She was very agitated and I was so embarrassed. We sat on the bus, among secular people. We knew that we had to look our best in order to make a *kiddush Hashem*, but she was making such a scene...

But I remembered: I had to respect Chaychie; she wasn't to blame.

Each time Chaychie was overwhelmed by her fear of the Germans, Mother would try to soothe her: "Chaychie, we don't live there anymore." Sometimes she spoke gently; other times, her tone was more strident.

One day, things got much worse. Mother quickly traveled by bus to a doctor in Tel Hashomer. The doctor became alarmed: "Rebbetzin, what happened?" he asked.

She pleaded with him. "Listen, Doctor! I have a Holocaust survivor staying in my house; please give me something for her!"

"I don't give medication like that," the doctor said. "I could be sent to prison."

Ultimately the doctor was not able to withstand Mother's pleas and he gave her medication. "Put it in her tea or her soup," he instructed.

At first, Chaychie did not know that she was taking medication. Mother did it very wisely: she purchased vitamin drops for our family and dripped some into each of our cups. Then she'd say, "Chaychie, do you want some? Look, we're taking vitamins. I am swallowing them and so is Esty. You can also."

And she agreed.

The medication had a positive effect on Chaychie; she calmed down and her mind grew clearer.

Chaychie came to us twice a year, for the *chagim*, and she always brought something expensive as a gift.

The visits were very good for her, but as soon as she returned to France and stopped taking her "vitamins" (because there was no one to follow up on her, even if she would have taken the medicine to France), she reverted right back to her old self.

Chaychie's stays in our house grew longer. At first, she was there only for *Yamim Tovim*. Then she stayed for two or three months, and finally, her visit extended to half a year.

Slowly, Mother taught her to be independent, to make purchases at the grocery, to choose what she needed. At one point, Mother decided that it would be better for Chaychie to live in her own apartment, which would help her feel good about herself. Mother was often out of the house and traveled frequently, and she preferred that Chaychie not remain alone in our large apartment.

Mother rented her a two and a half room apartment one floor beneath ours. Chaychie made her own grocery purchases and ate breakfast herself. At lunchtime she came up to Mother and stayed until the evening, when returned to her apartment.

When Mother wasn't home, my sister-in-law, the Sassover Rebbetzin in Kiryas Yismach Moshe, took over the job of supervising Chaychie (they lived across the street). That is a chapter of devotion and boundless *ahavas Yisrael* in and of itself.

Chaychie would sit in our house or in my sister-in-law's house during the afternoons, folding laundry and doing the mending. For us, it was a huge relief! We always told her, "Chaychie, we don't know how we would manage without you. You're our right hand." Indeed, she never folded a torn garment without fixing it right away. Her mending was of the highest quality. She also folded with wisdom, stacking things in age and size order. She was clearly a *balabuste,* and it was pleasant to be around her.

Chaychie was happy to help us; she didn't feel like such a burden on Mother. That was exactly the reason that Mother put her in charge of the laundry and the mending—to make her feel useful.

We would share all our purchases with her. She didn't like to go out because she was very suspicious of her surroundings. When we came home, we'd always show her what we had bought and asked her opinion. She could discern right away what had been bought in an expensive store and what was of lesser quality. She was happy with us when we found nice things, always *fargined* us, and gave us advice how to make the clothes look best.

Mother made sure she always looked good. Chaychie needed nothing for herself. "Who for? What for?" she'd say. But Mother invested in her, and after the fact Chaychie always enjoyed it.

We learned with time that we were not allowed to say a word about the past to Chaychie, because it triggered all her fears. We so much wanted to hear about Mother's family, who she had known very well, but we could not ask her.

We were not relaxed in her presence. We knew she was a poor

soul. Mother would remind us in what a dignified, special family Chaychie had been raised—and look at what she had become, totally dependent on others, without a single relative to speak of. Mother considered Chaychie to be her obligation in life, to guard over and her give her whatever she needed, with as much dignity as possible. We were all part of this noble effort.

The pure *chinuch* that Chaychie had absorbed in her parent's home in Poland was apparent. She was a *Yiras Hashem*, and very *frum*. She *davened* all the *tefillos* every day: first Shacharis, then the entire *sefer Tehillim*. By then it was almost time for lunch and in the evening she *davened* Minchah, Maariv, and *Kriyas Shema*. On Shabbos she would go to shul. Towards the end of her life she *davened* everything at home.

She was very organized and clean in her habits and her actions. She understood nuances and behaved tactfully. She spoke in a most refined manner, and never about other people. The purity of her speech was awe-inspiring.

Chaychie always returned to France when she was at her best. There, too, they agreed that it was good for Chaychie to live with us and that life in Eretz Yisrael suited her well. She was free here, traveling and living like a normal person.

Over the years of Chaychie's extended visits, Mother conducted a long correspondence with the French government, repeatedly requesting that they relinquish their custodianship over Chaychie.

"This story with the French has to finish," she would declare. The Lebels and Lederbergers helped her write the letters in fluent French. They were familiar with the details of the legal aspects and helped Mother compose her claims. Rebbetzin Miller was also in the picture the whole time, as was the Weiss family from Bnei Brak.

Mother claimed to the French that Chaychie would be better off among her brethren, people who respected her and had her best interests in mind. The French asked for proof of this claim, and piled endless obstacles in Mother's path. They didn't want to release Chaychie; as her custodians, the government received money from Germany and they only released to Chaychie as much as they decided she needed to live. Mother and her friends even raised money to pay for Chaychie's twice annual tickets to Eretz Yisrael.

At the end of a years-long battle of pleas, letters, ups and downs, the authorities set a date for psychological and psychiatric evaluations and for a hearing in court, after which they would decide whether to release Chaychie from their authority.

As the hearing approached Chaychie's friends were very anxious. They *davened* fervently that the French government would let Chaychie move to be with other Jews and live independently in Eretz Yisrael.

Mother planned to accompany Chaychie to France for the hearing. She prepared her for the evaluations, warning her that there would be extensive questioning and she would have to answer complicated questions, because the French government would be trying to trip her up.

The date set for the evaluations fell two days before the bar mitzvah of Mother's grandson, Rabbi Yoel Teitelbaum, the son of my brother, the Sassover Rebbe.

Mother did not desist from her plans to travel. In addition, a complicated turn of events took place: she began to feel unwell for the third time. Only four years earlier, she had recovered from her eye illness, and now she began to feel sick again. She was very afraid that, as the doctor had told her at the time, the illness was spreading to her liver.

Despite all that, Mother declared that she wasn't getting busy with anything else until after the hearing at the French court.

That was not Mother's usual way of thinking. She had never fled from challenges or evaded what she had to do. But here, it was not a matter of postponing or pushing it away. She simply wanted to see Chaychie settled before she started with tests and treatments—there was no way to know how much time that could take.

Before the trip, she purchased a wig and an elegant blue hat for Chaychie so that she would appear impressive in France. Thus, with Mother unwell, but full of motivation and drive to take on the challenge, she departed with Chaychie to France.

Two days of meetings and hearings passed in Paris. A psychologist and a psychiatrist conducted their evaluations, which were followed by a hearing presided over by a French judge, Mrs. Toledano, who apparently was Jewish.

Between meetings, Mother and Chaychie went on a shopping trip in Paris' large department stores to purchase a kerchief, a scarf, or some other item of clothing. Chaychie had good taste, and in one of the stores she noticed a woman trying on a scarf. She advised the woman, "I think this scarf suits you better than that one."

The woman was pleased with Chaychie's recommendation and heeded her advice, purchasing the second scarf that suited her better.

When Mother and Chaychie came to the meeting with the psychiatrist, they discovered that she was the woman from the store! There was no need to say too much; the woman had seen Chaychie functioning perfectly, and was ready to issue a warm recommendation. "There's no doubt we can lift the custodianship!"

The hearings continued and, among other things, Chaychie was asked: "Do you know that you are going to live with the Rebbetzin, who manages a yeshivah (*kollel*); and she will certainly use your money for her institutions (a totally groundless claim, of course)?"

Chaychie replied so emphatically that she left them all openmouthed and speechless. Mother also delivered a short speech in fluent French. She explained how important it was for Chaychie to live in her own society, among Jews who loved her, to whom she was important, and that she would be treated most respectfully by them.

The speech apparently impressed the judge, who ruled that if Chaychie would live with such a woman, then it would undoubtedly be the best place for her.

French was not Mother's first language. She had only lived in France for a short time (after the war) and yet, she had the confidence and the courage to speak in clear and fluent French, to the extent that a hostile, gentile court, unwilling to give up on a lucrative asset such as Chaychie, agreed with her heartfelt words.

They did not receive the final ruling on the spot: the letter would be sent after some time. In actuality, it was delayed for months and when it finally arrived with the approval to lift the custodianship, Mrs. Rachel Lebel was no longer among the living. She and her husband had invested so much effort over the years in releasing Chaychie, and they certainly had a great *zechus*.

As the meetings and hearings came to an end, during their final hours in France, Chaychie began to feel unwell. She was vomiting incessantly, and Mother was having a very hard time. At first, she didn't know what to do. She'd promised to attend the bar mitzvah; she could not be delayed. Furthermore, if Chaychie would be hospitalized in France it certainly would not bode well on the final decision.

Finally Mother turned to Chaychie and said, "It's a short flight. We're going home." Mother equipped herself with a large number of bags and traveled with Chaychie to the airport. She updated Mrs. Burstein that Chaychie was not feeling well and asked her to come to the airport and take Chaychie straight to the hospital so Mother could get to the bar mitzvah.

I just want to mention, in passing, the unbelievable friendship between Mother and Mrs. Esther Burstein. Through Mrs. Burstein's job as the bookkeeper of Yismach Moshe, the two became extremely close. I have no way to adequately praise and express my appreciation for her. Hashem should pay Esther's reward and grant her a long life, nachas from her family, health and success until 120.

Mother was busy with Chaychie the entire journey. She pulled out a bag, and as soon as it filled, she discarded it and started a new one...

Mrs. Burstein was waiting at the airport, and took Chaychie to Tel Hashomer Hospital, where she was diagnosed with an intestinal obstruction. Mrs. Burstein sat with her all night, and then we spent a few days at her bedside until Chaychie recovered (until the next time.)

Meanwhile, Mother hurried home to dress and get ready for the bar mitzvah. When she arrived she told everyone that she had a very good feeling and that she thought they had impressed whoever needed to be impressed.

Only after her return, did Mother go through the necessary tests to discover that she had taken ill the third time.

Joyous times in our house were times of crisis for Chaychie, who was usually positive and upbeat. For her it was a time to introspect and to ask herself: Who are you? What will become of you?

She would refuse to come with us to *simchahs* and we had a hard time persuading her. In the end she would come and enjoy herself.

Chaychie also joined us when the whole family traveled to America for the marriage of the oldest son of the Sassover Rebbe, Rav Chananyah Yom Tov Lipa Teitelbaum, *shlita*, to the granddaughter of the Beirach Moshe of Satmar, *zt"l*. My brother, the Rebbe's family, stayed at the home of the wonderful Kosovitz family, and Chaychie stayed with them as an integral part of the family.

I remember the day of my wedding. Excitement hung in the air. My sister-in-law and her children from America were staying in our home. There was the normal hustle and bustle of a wedding day and…Chaychie. She was refusing to get dressed for the wedding.

It was a hard day for her. To observe the warm, vibrant family—and where was she? What was her future?

Already wearing my gown, I pleaded with her. "Chaychie, I'll help you get dressed. Please, come and share my *simchah*."

The hands on the watch moved forward. The *mechuteineste* had already arrived at our house, as had the *chasan's* grandmother, and I was busy with Chaychie. I was so distracted that I forgot to put on the earrings my mother-in-law had given me…

Finally, after endless pleading, Chaychie agreed to come. She had a wonderful time dancing with everyone, and sitting as they danced around her.

As my mother's youngest child, I felt a special obligation towards her. I was happy on the one hand that Mother was not alone, because Chaychie was in the house, but on the other hand, it was a big responsibility, and not a simple one, for Mother.

It became a matter of routine in our family: whenever we came to visit Mother (and after her passing, all those who came to my brother's house were informed), the first thing we had to do was say hello to Chaychie. We knocked, asked how she was doing and received her good wishes. This applied to children, grandchildren, neighbors, and acquaintances. Even the *chassidim* and visitors to my brother's home knew that they had to respect her and go over to her to receive a *brachah*.

There was always a dish with candies that Chaychie made sure to have on hand for visitors. Her table was covered with a pretty tablecloth and the house was clean and well-tended. There was a cleaning lady once a week, but the rest of the time, Chaychie maintained the house alone.

Anyone who emerged from her house was escorted with her *brachos*: "*Gei gezunterheit, zei gebencht*," be healthy, be blessed. Whenever someone did something kind for her, she would thank them and say, "*Zolst du zein gebencht*," you should be blessed. Her words were full of gratitude.

She spent many hours in the homes of my mother and brother, and she was always surrounded by little children. It didn't bother her at all. Sometimes she was asked, "Chaychie, doesn't the tumult bother you?"

And she would reply, "Of course not. It's the *nachas* and it's wonderful. Why should it bother me?"

The children felt comfortable around her and would snuggle up to her as though she was their loving grandmother.

On Shabbos and *Yamim Tovim* she would be my brother's guest, together with my Mother, and received all the honor and respect possible.

Chaychie fell ill. She felt worse and was given medication that halted the progression of the disease. We felt terrible for her.

When Mother fell ill with her final illness, we didn't tell Chaychie anything, but the deterioration was rapid. It is impossible to describe Chaychie's anguish when Mother passed away—she was her whole world! (When Mrs. Rachel Lebel passed away, Chaychie was also very grief-stricken over the passing of someone who was so close and good to her.)

Chaychie felt overwhelmed with pain and loss. "Why was the Rebbetzin taken? Why not me?" she would moan.

HaKadosh Baruch Hu did not abandon Chaychie. Mother's shoes were filled by my sister-in-law, the Sassover Rebbetzin, in an exceptional way. She devoted herself to Chaychie in a way that I cannot even describe.

When Chaychie was ill, there were ups and downs. On Succos she was taken to the hospital, and my sister-in-law stayed with her the entire time. I was also there part of the time; I had left my family at home to be with her in the hospital.

We couldn't leave her alone because she was very afraid and suspicious of strangers. The hospital staff could not get over the devotion we displayed towards Chaychie.

When she was discharged and returned to her house, Chaychie needed complicated treatment, and my sister-in-law administered it in the most caring way possible.

We could not hire a foreign aide to do the job because of Chaychie's fears. My sister-in-law didn't want us to in any case, as she wanted to care for Chaychie herself.

When my sister-in-law traveled abroad, Chaychie stayed in my home for several weeks. She was also a guest at the home of my brother, Rav Moshe Teitelbum, and my sister-in-law, Rebbetzin Miriam. She and her children cared for Chaychie with such dignity and kindness. They repeatedly emphasized to her how lucky they were and what an honor it was for them to host her.

In the years when Chaychie was healthy, I could go out to work or shop and leave her in my house for a few hours. But in her final years, we had to remain with her at all times.

I remember the time I brought a neighbor to my house to receive a *brachah* from Chaychie. I forgot to warn her ahead of time, and the neighbor innocently began to ask her where she came from. Chaychie turned her head, withdrew into herself and refused to continue talking.

We couldn't predict when "it" would come, when she would be overcome with fear and sadness. We always felt the sense of missed opportunity, because we were so close to someone who knew Mother's family well, but she refused to talk. It took her back to "then," and she would become frozen with fear that "they are coming."

During Chaychie's final two years, the fears came on their own, without any triggers. "Here, they're coming, I hear them coming, he's bringing them."

We would try to soothe her. "Chaychie, you know that's not true!" But it was useless.

My sister-in-law showered Chaychie with boundless love. "You're my mother, my grandmother, you are everything to me," she would tell her. We made sure to frequently express our love for her. Chaychie was enveloped with love and attention, honor and admiration, from every member of our families. It was clear that she was *ours,* unconditionally. We had inherited this from Mother, who brought Chaychie into our lives as an obligation and as a great *zechus.*

As she aged, the years took their toll. Nevertheless, even the babies wanted to sit on her lap. Even though strangers who came to the house were sometimes frightened at first, they quickly got swept up into the atmosphere of respect and admiration that we all accorded her.

At family weddings, the *mechutanim* all knew that Chaychie was at the center. The entire family danced around her and for her. She would enjoy this even though for hours beforehand, she would refuse to get ready or participate in the *simchah* at all...

Often, guests and *mechutanim* would ask: "Which side exactly is the grandmother from?" We would evade the question and present it as fact: she's a dear, important grandmother to us. That was the end of the story.

Chaychie suffered for several years from her ailment, until it became necessary to operate. The operation needed to be repeated every so often. At one point, Chaychie moved into the same building as my brother, the Rebbe, because she was so dependent on my sister-in-law for her treatment.

My brother's daughters slept in Chaychie's apartment in shifts. The oldest daughter at home slept with Chaychie; after she married, the next one had the privilege of this mitzvah. It was self-understood and did not need to be spoken about. This arrangement involved a regular commitment, because when evening came, Chaychie would wait for whichever daughter it was to accompany her home, and then that girl would lose out on the evening hours with the family.

Chaychie's living room became the private bedroom of whichever girl was sleeping there at the time. She could decorate the room with knickknacks and photos, and invite friends to study or sleep over. This way, Chaychie was part of the life of the younger generation. Friends would ask how she was doing; every married grandchild brought over a photo of the couple and the house was filled with pictures.

Chaychie took breakfast and supper, prepared by my sister-in-law, home to eat herself. All the daughters and daughters-in-law helped out, while the *bochurim* would carry her chair up to the Rebbe's house.

In her final years, Chaychie had trouble walking. When

necessary, we would order a car for her so she would be comfortable. Everyone took her needs into consideration— when she couldn't go out and we had to attend a wedding, acquaintances would keep her company while we were gone. It became part and parcel of all our lives—we were all responsible for Chaychie.

In her last year, she became completely dependent. While still in France, she had broken her pelvis, and now, the pain resurfaced. This made her condition more serious. Ultimately, she began to sleep in my sister-in-law's house instead of going downstairs to her own. In other words: she moved in, and got the best room in the house. The children moved to the sofa in the dining room.

Chaychie was never alone for that last year. If it wasn't the daughters or daughters-in-law, then friends or wives of the *chassidim* came to be with Chaychie.

She was hospitalized periodically. The family doctor was very dedicated and my sister-in-law would consult with him often. During her final hospitalization, Chaychie was terrified of the medical staff and we didn't leave her alone for a moment.

Two days before my sister-in-law was to marry off her daughter, she had to take Chaychie to the hospital. I came to take over so my sister-in-law could leave to get ready for the *simchah*. For two days straight I remained at her bedside, and my clothes for the wedding were brought to the hospital.

I tried to ask the doctor to release Chaychie so she could attend the wedding, but he refused. On the morning of the wedding, my sister-in-law came to the hospital and set firm facts down before the doctor: there was no way that Chaychie would remain in the hospital. She had to attend the wedding. We couldn't have a wedding without her. "This is our grandmother," she declared.

At first, the staff tried to argue with us. "She's not your grandmother," they hedged. But we didn't let up and we took her to the wedding. She thoroughly enjoyed herself.

The hospital's social worker could not get over it. "I wish other survivors would get such treatment."

When Chaychie's condition worsened and she could no longer be helped medically, my sister-in-law preferred that she remain home and spend the rest of her life among people who she knew and who loved her, instead of the hospital that she so hated and feared.

Then came the nights when she would speak with the souls of her departed loved ones. It was a frightening scene; we were afraid that she was dying and going to meet her family in the Upper World.

Chaychie was in my house for a week and each night, we heard her speaking with her good friend, "Leah'le," with her mother and other dear ones. I was afraid that she was leaving the world, and I would shake her and say, "Chaychie, Chaychie, are you with me?"

She didn't answer me, she just repeatedly *bentsched* me, as if from afar, "*Yevarechcha* Hashem *veyishmeracha*...again and again..."

On Friday, 2 Tammuz, Chaychie lit four *yahrtzeit* candles for her parents, brother, and sister who perished on 3 Tammuz, which fell on Shabbos that year.

The names of her loved ones were her father, Reb Yechiel Alter ben Reb Yehudah Leib, *Hy"d*; her mother, Aidel bas Reb Mordechai Dovid, *Hy"d*; her brother, Mordechai Dovid ben Reb Yechiel Alter, *Hy"d*; and her sister, Devorah bas Reb Yechiel Alter, *Hy"d*.

(Another brother, Yaakov Yitzchak ben Reb Yechiel Alter, *Hy"d*, was killed on 26 Sivan, and her aunt, Fradel bas Reb Mordechai Dovid, *Hy"d*, perished on 6 Tammuz. Chaychie observed these *yahrtzeits* each year.)

That Friday, 2 Tammuz, the candles burned in her room, telling the story of a family that was wiped out without a trace.

Except for Chaychie.

On Shabbos morning, 3 Tammuz, 5772/2012, before my sister-in-law went down to shul, she offered Chaychie a drink, which she accepted. She made the *brachah*, and unlike her usual habit, she said it out loud. The Rebbe, who was still home, heard the *brachah* and answered, "Amen."

The Rebbe's daughter-in-law, Mrs. Rechy Teitelbaum, remained at home and cared for Chaychie. May her good deeds be a *zechus* for her.

A few minutes later, Chaychie returned her soul to its Maker, on the same day as the *yahrtzeit* of her family, at the age of 91.

The candles all flickered around her. The scene was both moving and chilling. It seemed as though her family had come to welcome her and help her make the transition into the world where all is good.

That's how this dear soul departed this world, after giving up her entire life for her friend. For us, she was a paragon of *mesirus nefesh* of one *bas Yisrael* to another.

Through giving to Chaychie, Mother taught us that there is no limit to dedication, no limit to *ahavas Yisrael. Mah Hu [Ribbono Shel Olam] rachum, af atah rachum.*

May Chaychie's soul rest in Gan Eden—Chaya bas Reb Yechiel Alter, *a"h*.

I Sing, Because My Heart Overflows

Mother's soul was a fount of *ahavas Hashem*, longing and yearning, of lofty, noble values. At various opportunities, she penned her emotions and wrote wondrous songs in Yiddish. She wrote them for her children or grandchildren, or for the members of the Kosovitz family, her benefactors, when they needed them for school. The songs are varied and cover a range of subjects, based on what was needed at the time, and she expressed herself in a most talented fashion.

The Holy Zeideh, the Yitav Lev of Sighet, *zy"a*

אוי ווי זאל איך אנהייבן	How can I begin
און וואס זאל איך אייך דערציילן	What can I tell you
פון דעם גרויסן הייליגן זיידן	About the great, holy grandfather
דער "ייטב לב' וואס איז שוין לאנג אין גן-עדן	The "Yitav Lev" who is already long in Gan Eden
און דאס דארפט איר וויסן	And this you must know
א זון פון ר' אליעזר ניסן	That he was the son of Rav Eliezer Nissan
א צווייג פון דעם הערליכן בוים	A branch of the magnificent tree
א אייניקל פון ר' משה טייטלבוים	A grandson of Rav Moshe Teitelbaum
וואס צוט זיין יחוס פון גרויסן רמ"א	Whose lineage goes back to the great Rema
וואס אזא פוסק איז שוין מער נישטא	Who was a *posek* the likes of which has never been seen since
נאך אין דראהביטש פון קינדוויייז אן	Still in Drohobitz, in the days of his youth
האט מען געזעהן אז דא וואקסט א גאון	It was apparent that (the Yitav Lev) was destined for greatness
אויך זיין התמדה איז געווען גאר גרויס	His diligence was outstanding
נישט קיין וואנדער וואס פון דעם קינד איז ארויס	It was no wonder that this child grew into the giant that he was
שפעטער נעבן זיין גרויסן זיידן	Later, he basked in the presence of his holy grandfather
האט ער זיך טאקע כסדר געהייבן	And rose steadily
און אין די הייליגע אווירה	In the lofty atmosphere
געשטויגן אין תורה און אין יראה	He made great strides in Torah and *Yiras Shamayim*
מיט טאלטשעווער רב'ס טאכטער האט ער חתונה געהאט	Married the daughter of the Tolchover Rebbe
און פיל מיטגעמאכט	And suffered so much during that time
געליטן קעלט און הונגער	From cold and hunger.
איז דאך נאך מיר וואנדער	So it is therefore so remarkable
אז דאך געלערנט טאג און נאכט	That even at such times he learned Torah day and night
געטובבלט זיך דארט אין א קאלטן טייך	And immersed in the freezing waters of the river

ווי ער וואלט געווען פאכיך, ווייך...	As though it was soft and warm
אזוי איז אויסגעוואקסן דער גרויסער ריז	And that's how that giant of giants grew
וואס תורה און עבודה איז אים געוועהן זיס	With Torah and *avodas Hashem* dear to him above all
געוועהן א רב אין א סאך קהילות	He served as the rav in many communities
איבעראל אויפגעטוהן, גרויסע פעולות	And wherever he went, great things would happen
ביז ענדליך קיין סיגעט אנגעקומען	Until he reached the city of Sighet
דער רבנות-שטעלע דארט אנגענומען	And became the Rav there
א גרויסע ישיבה דארט אויפגעשטעלט	He established a large yeshivah
מיט הונדערטע תלמידים פון דער גאנצער וועלט	Where hundreds of students learned from all over the world,
פאר כלל ישראל פלעגט פועל'ן ישועות	And he effected *yeshuos* for Klal Yisrael
געבענטשט זיי מיט פרנסה און רפואות	And blessed them with *parnassah* and healing
תרמ"ג ו' אלול האט ער זיך פון דער וועלט געזעגנט	On 6 Elul 5643 he departed from this world
איבערלאזנדיג פאר'יתומט די גאנצע געגנט	Leaving behind an orphaned region
נאר א ירושה איז דאך געבליבן	But there was a valuable inheritance
די וויכטיקע ספרים וואס ער האט געשריבן	His important *sefarim* that he wrote
און זיין חשובע זון דער ממלא מקום	And his holy son and successor
דער "קדושת יום טוב" די וועלטס קרוין	The Kedushas Yom Tov, the crown of the world
נאך אים זיין אייניקל רבנו יואל	And then his grandson, Rabbeinu Yoel of Satmar
וואס זיצן אלע צוזאמען און אויבערשטן אוהל	Who are all seated together in the Tent Above
הלואי זאלן זיי אויסבעטן משיח צדקנו	*Halevai* they should *daven* for the arrival of Mashiach
טאקע, בקרוב, בקרוב בימינו!	Speedily, soon in our day!

Song for the Fireman Costume – Purim 5751

איך בין א פייער לעשער	I am a firefighter
איך דערלאנג די העכסטע דעכער	Climbing high on the roofs
שטענדיג דארף איך זיין א זריז	I have to be quick
כדי צו פארמיידן מענטשנ׳ס צרות	To save people from trouble
און וואס שנעלער גיסן וואסער	To spray water as fast as I can
נישט קוקענדיג אז כ׳ווער א נאסער	And not to pay attention that I'm getting wet
וויל צו ראטעווען מענטשנ׳ס לעבן	So I can save lives.
האב איך זיך אוועקגעגעבן	I am *moser nefesh*
אויף די לייטער הויער, הויך	Climbing on ladders
שנעל געשיקט און מיט כח	Swiftly and energetically
לויף איך ארויף און אראפ	Up and down I go
צו ראטעווען מענטשנ׳ס גאב	To save other people's belongings
און בעיקר יעדע נפש חיה	And mostly human lives
ראטעווען פון דעם פייער	That I save from fires.
אוי באשעפער גיב הצלחה	Oh, Hashem, bless me that I should succeed
אין די וויכטיגע מלאכה	In this important job!
און איך האב נאך איין בקשה	And I have one more request:
אז ברענען זאל דער גרויסער רשע	That the evil *rasha* should burn in the fire
סאדאם חוסיין, סאדאם חוסיין	You, Saddam Hussein
דיין מפלה וויל איך שוין זעהן	Your downfall should come about quickly

און איד יעדן איד'נס הארץ	And may every Jew's heart
קיינמאל זאל נישט זיין שווארץ	Never become black
ברענענען זאל און זיי א פייער פון תורה	The flames of Torah should always burn
פארן הייליגן בורא זאלן זיי האבן מורא	And they should fear only the holy Creator
דעמאלס וועט בודאי קומען די ישועה	And then the *yeshuah* will certainly come
אלא יידישע שונאים וועלן גיין אויף א תליה	And all those enemies of Am Yisrael should be hung.

The Secret is Revealed

A story set against the backdrop of bitter reality.

Poland, 1943. The war is storming around us in full force. The hatred of Am Yisrael is burning furiously and mounting from day to day. The cities and towns in Poland are becoming Judenrein one after another! Ghettos and camps are being established, and the trains speed ahead, their cars loaded with exhausted, starving Yidden.

Entire communities, pure, holy souls, are annihilated overnight. Where are they being taken? Where are they going? To the unknown, to a terrible end. Auschwitz, Majdanek, or Belzec. The heart senses that it does not bode well; who knows if the evildoers will leave even a remnant...

In one such car is the B. family. Four little children surround the parents; the mother grasps her youngest child, trying to soothe his wailing as he pleads for a bit of water to drink. With sorrowful eyes, the father gazes at the scene; suddenly, he turns to his wife and says, "Let's try and save at least one of our children, so that there will be a memory of our family." But how can he do this? Suddenly, he remembers a small, sharp knife that miraculously remained in his pocket. He grabs the knife with trembling hands and begins working around the little window. He is covered in a cold sweat, as he feels the opening widen. At once, he lifts his three-year-old daughter, Rivka'le, and wraps her in a warm, thick rag that he happened to grab when they left the house. He quickly writes on a scrap of paper: This is Rivka B.

In a flash, he throws the bundle out of the narrow opening, as his lips murmur, *"Yevarchech Hashem veyishmerech..."*

Rivka'le remains lying on the ground, wrapped in the rag, not understanding what is happening to her.

Divide Providence sends a Polish farmwoman past the site, and she notices the little bundle. Immediately, she understands what must have transpired. She takes the child to her, and grips her fearfully—but her feelings of compassion do not allow her to toss the child to a certain death.

Weeks and months pass; the gentile woman grows to love the child, and Rivka'le lacks for nothing. Maybe something will remain of the B. family after all...

But one day, a tragic Sunday, a group of people come to the house to spend time. The farmer who owns the house get drunk and begins to speak about fire and water...until he reveals the secret that there is a Jewish child hiding in his home.

His friends are true enemies of the Jews, and they immediately run to the police station and report what they have heard. By the next morning, Rivka'le is no longer.

Listen to what happened,
The Jewish fate caught up with her as well.
Already by dawn,
They took the child from the house,
Indifferently, in cold blood,
They took her deep into the forest
And shot her in the head.
Innocent Jewish blood was spilled.
Oh Hashem, avenge
That pure, precious soul
And avenge every other Jewish child,
Because the wound is still open and so very painful.

The Child-Adult

פלעגט די באבע פון מיין באבע דערציילן,	My grandmother's grandmother used to tell
מעשיות פון דעם עָבר אסאך און א שיעור,	Many stories of the past
ווי מען האט געלעבט אמאל	How they once used to live
און וואס ס'האט פאסירט אין דער וועלט.	And how life was in the world.
ביי די קינדער פון ישראל ארום דער יידישע געצעלט,	For Klal Yisrael around the world
ווען פון צאר אין רוסלאנד א באפעל איז ארויס,	When the Czar in Russia issued a decree
אז יעדעס אינגל פון יידישן הויז,	That every Jewish child
מוז אין די גוישע שולע גיין	Had to study in a non-Jewish school
איז געווארן א גרויס געוויין	A hue and cry arose
ביז א עצה מ'האט געפונען	Until a solution was found
חתונה מאכן קליינע קינדער האט מען באגינען	They began to marry off the little children
ווייל ערליכע יידן זענען זיי אלע געוועזן	Who were all G-d-fearing Yidden
און מורא געהאט האבן זיי וואס קען געשעהן	And were afraid of what could happen
מיט גויים צו זיצן אויף איין באנק	If they would sit side by side with non-Jewish students.
די נשמה קען דערפון ווערן קראנק	Their souls could get sick and damaged.
פלעגט די באבע פון מיין באבע וויַיטער דערציילן	My grandmother's grandmother continued to relate
אזוי ווי מיט פערד און וואגן איז מען געפארן מיַילן	That once they traveled with horse and wagon very far,
מאנכעס מאל אין גרויסע הוצן	Sometimes it was very hot
און מען פלעגט טאקע שטארק שוויצן	And they would sweat a lot
זוכט מען א טרינק וואסער	Looking to drink a bit of water
צו דערלייכטן די נשמה	To revive themselves
שווער אבער צו טרעפן א נחמה	However it was hard to find solace
ווייל נישט קיין קיוסק און נישט קיין ברונעם	Because there was neither a shop nor a well on the way
קען מען ערגעץ וואו געפונען	So where would they find water?

נא אט לויפט פארביי א שאנס

Just then runs by

א יידיש יינגל א גאט בחנ׳טס

A charming Yiddishe child

יינגעלע, יינגל בעט מען פון אים

Yingele, little boy, they ask him

טו א חסד און טרעף א ברונעם

Do a *chessed* and find a well

טו א טובה און ברענג וואסער

Do a favor and bring us water

וויל מיין צונג וויל זיין א נאסער

Because our tongues are sticking to the roofs of our mouths

במילא ענטפערט ער

The child replies:

טא א קלײנע, אבער א יינגעלע בין איך שוין נישט מער

I may be little, but I'm no longer a child

נאר א יונגערמאן ווי עס גיהער

But rather an *avreich*

נעכטן האב איך חתונה גיהאט

I got married last night

כדי אפגעהיטן ווערן פונ׳ם שמד

To be spared the decree

אין די גויישע שולע נישט דארפן באזוכן

So that I don't have to go to the gentile school

מיין יודישע נשמה פון אלעם בײַן באשיצן

And this way I will protect my soul

אזוי האבן ייִדן פון יענע דורות

That's how the Yidden in previous generations were,
They would seek all kinds of ways and ideas to cling to their roots

געזוכט וועגן נישט אבגערוסן ווערן פונ׳ם שורש

A Father's Plea for His Hungry Children

אין א ווינקל איינגעבויגן	In a corner, bent over
מיט דעם פנים שטארק פארצויגן	His face very tense
מיט הכנעה, זייער פארשעמט	With submission and shame,
הויבט ר' יצחק צום הימל די הענט	Reb Yitzchak raises his hands to the Heavens
מיט א שטארקע צובראכענע שטימע	And in a broken voice
בעט ר' יצחק זיין תפילה תמימה	Offers up a pure prayer
זאל ער טאקע בעטן ברויט	Should he really ask for bread
ווייל גרויס איז שוין די נויט?	Because it is already so very desperate?
איז עס דען א גרויסער וואונדער	Is it then any wonder
זיינע קינדער שוין בלוי פון הונגער?	That his children have already turned blue from hunger?
ווי קען א טאטע דאס צוזעהן	How can a father look
ווי זיינע קינדער פון הונגער אויסגיין?	While his children are dying from hunger?
שיק באשעפער פאר זיי עסן	Hashem, send food for them
וועלן זיי דיר נישט פארגעסן	And they will not forget You forever,
דיר א שבח אנצוגעבן	They will praise You
בקדושה וטהרה צו לעבן	And live in holiness and purity
דיינע מצוות בשמחה מקיים זיין	They will carry out the mitzvos joyfully
ובזכות זה צו דער גאולה זוכה זיין	And in this *zechus* they will merit the Redemption
א הארציגע תפילה באגלייט מיט טרערן	A warm *tefillah*, accompanied by tears
זאל פון דיר היי'ליגער באשעפער דערהערט ווערן	That from You, Hashem, it should be heard
דער ביהמ"ק זאל בקרוב ווידער געבויעט ווערן	The news that the Bais Hamikdash is being rebuilt.

In Eternal Memory

The moving and remarkable stories of my mother, the Sassover Rebbetzin, remained untold for decades. Now we have finally merited the privilege of publishing her memoirs in English. At the end of the *sefer*, we included stories and vignettes portraying her unique personality and the strength she displayed as she navigated her way through her tumultuous life — with joy and spirit, for the sake of Hashem's name, because in whatever she did, she saw Him.

This is an opportunity to mention the names of my unforgettable loved ones:

My dear first wife, who stood beside me throughout her life, raising our children and imbuing them with Torah and *Yiras Shamayim*. She also helped me record my mother's words, and encouraged me to publish them. May Hashem reward her in the Upper World.

Rebbetzin Chana Mindel, *a"h*

bas **HaRav HaGaon R' Eliyahu Yehoshua Geldzahler**, *shlita*
who passed away on 26 Sivan 5771/2011 at the age of 57.

The souls of **my dear children**, who returned their pure souls to their Maker:

My dear son, **Shloma**, *z"l*
Who passed away on 7 Shevat 5774/2014 at the age of 29

My dear son, **Reuven Dov**, *z"l*
who passed away on 11 Iyar 5762/2002 at the age of 18

My dear son, **Yekusiel Yehudah**, *z"l*
Who passed away on Hoshanah Rabbah, 21 Tishrei, 5749/1988 at the age of 2 months.

HaRav Chanoch Henoch Teitelbaum
Son of **the Sassover Rebbe**, *zy"a*

Acknowledgements

Thank you to all those who graciously helped
complete this book:

My sister **Rebbetzin Esther Rabinowitz**, *tlita*

My nephew, **HaRav Yochanan Teitelbaum**, *shlita*

And those who helped work on the book,

Tfutza Publications

Reb Aharon Flohr

The devoted *gabbai*, **Reb Kasriel Mayer**

May they be blessed by Hashem, and may the merit of
our righteous parents and grandparents protect them
and bless them with an abundance of *brachah*, success,
nachas and *siyata diShamaya* in all their endeavors.

HaRav Chanoch Henoch Teitelbaum
Son of the **Sassover Rebbe**, *zecher tzaddik livrachah*